Easter 2009

fr...

PENGUIN BOO

Co

COUNTRY
CHURCHES

*Simon
Jenkins*

English 🐧 *Journeys*

PENGUIN BOOKS

Published by the Penguin Group
Penguin Books Ltd, 80 Strand, London WC2R 0RL, England
Penguin Group (USA) Inc., 375 Hudson Street, New York, New York 10014, USA
Penguin Group (Canada), 90 Eglinton Avenue East, Suite 700, Toronto, Ontario, Canada M4P 2Y3
(a division of Pearson Penguin Canada Inc.)
Penguin Ireland, 25 St Stephen's Green, Dublin 2, Ireland
(a division of Penguin Books Ltd)
Penguin Group (Australia), 250 Camberwell Road, Camberwell, Victoria 3124, Australia
(a division of Pearson Australia Group Pty Ltd)
Penguin Books India Pvt Ltd, 11 Community Centre, Panchsheel Park, New Delhi – 110 017, India
Penguin Group (NZ), 67 Apollo Drive, Rosedale, North Shore 0632, New Zealand
(a division of Pearson New Zealand Ltd)
Penguin Books (South Africa) (Pty) Ltd, 24 Sturdee Avenue, Rosebank, Johannesburg 2196, South Africa

Penguin Books Ltd, Registered Offices: 80 Strand, London WC2R 0RL, England

www.penguin.com

This selection taken from *England's Thousand Best Churches*, first published by Allen Lane 1999
Published in Penguin Books 2009
1

Copyright © Simon Jenkins, 1999
All rights reserved

Set by Rowland Phototypesetting Ltd, Bury St Edmunds, Suffolk
Printed in England by Clays Ltd, St Ives plc

ISBN: 978-0-141-19088-4

www.greenpenguin.co.uk

Penguin Books is committed to a sustainable future
for our business, our readers and our planet.
The book in your hands is made from paper
certified by the Forest Stewardship Council.

Contents

Berkshire

Langley Marish

This is for connoisseur church-hunters. We are not just in Slough but in a suburban backstreet of Slough, minutes from the A4 and five from the M4. Cars are everywhere. The setting could hardly be less promising. Yet here lies one of the gems of English Church art, the Kedermister pew and library.

The church is basically medieval, a nave, chancel and large north aisle and chapel. A restored 15th-century screen divides nave and chancel. The floor includes a number of 14th-century tiles and a Green Man lurks on the north side of the chancel arcade. But all this is subsidiary to the work of Sir John Kedermister, whose alterations to the church in the early years of the 17th century are the glory of Langley. The Jacobeans could be as generous patrons of parish churches as were their 15th-century forebears.

Kedermisters were keepers of the Crown park of Langley in the Tudor period. The family discharged this task so well that by 1626 John Kedermister had been given a lease on the park and a knighthood. He not only rebuilt much of the church and endowed the adjacent almshouses, he also imitated many enlightened patrons in buying and installing a parish library, one of the few to survive. He died without heir in 1631 and the estate passed first to the Seymours and then to the Harveys. The latter's monuments feature prominently in the Kedermister Chapel.

The older Kedermister memorial in the chancel is a late-Tudor work, extravagant with strapwork and heraldry. Some of this is painted as a mural on the wall. Father and grandfather with their wives occupy two panels, kneeling in prayer with their families beneath them. The future Sir John is the eldest of the group of thirteen on the left. A similar memorial to his father-in-law is in Dorney church.

Sir John's most extensive changes were to the south transept, which is raised on a family vault and reached up a flight of steps. It is furnished with one of the most delightful works of Jacobean design, the Kedermister pew. This is approached through a Gothic Coade stone screen inserted by the Harvey family at the end of the 18th century, apparently keen to make their own mark on the work of their predecessor. Today it is the Harvey monuments that loom over the old chapel, in a variety of Georgian and Victorian funerary styles. The earliest, to David and Elizabeth Harvey of 1791, has a woman representing religion, holding a book and leaning on an urn.

The south wall is filled with the Kedermister pew. Such installations were a Reformation innovation. Previously the wealthy of the parish might sit in special seats in the chancel but they remained part of the congregation. As chantries and chapels were abolished, many

2

were converted into private boxes, often reusing old screens for this purpose. As at Rycote (Oxon) these boxes might occupy most of the nave, confining the tenantry to the back benches or the gallery. But most pews were in some way open to the church, their owners signifying community leadership by their presence in the body of the church.

Not so the Kedermisters. Their pew is sealed from the church by a screen and ceiling. It might be the women's balcony of a mosque. The screen's upper panels are filled with lattice-work grilles, enabling the occupants to see the pulpit, though not the chancel. Private access was by a door at the rear. The screen is wooden but painted to look like marble, with panels and bosses, and topped by a Latin text and strapwork crest. The ceiling has ventilation panels. Above in the towering south window are the Kedermister arms in stained glass. Lest any family member thinks themselves too aloof from worship, Sir John had eyes (of God) painted throughout the interior.

The library is behind the pew. This is a small cabinet entirely walled with panels on which are painted cartouches, saints and landscape scenes. The panels open to reveal over 200 books, a collection completed by the 1630s and including valuable medieval manuscripts. These are no longer stored in the building. Such costly collections would normally have been confined to a squire's private library. This was a generous donation to the parish and remains the property of a local trust. The insides of the panels include portraits of Sir John and his wife and catalogues of the contents. It is the jewel of Slough.

Cheshire

Nantwich

ST MARY
Octagonal tower, medieval stall canopies

Nantwich, once capital of the Cheshire salt industry, is a discreet market town with a well-designed pedestrian area at its heart. Here the church overlooks a small green that gives onto the churchyard. Though the exterior is darkened by the poor ageing quality of Cheshire sandstone, the church's interior is the glory of the county. Apart from George Gilbert Scott's 19th-century west front, the building is essentially Decorated in form, a thrilling composition.

Crowning the exterior is the octagonal crossing tower, rising majestic over an enveloping canopy of trees. Beneath Perpendicular battlements and pinnacles, the bell-openings have Decorated ogee hoods. Most of the window tracery is also Decorated, either Reticulated or Intersecting, that in the chancel enriched with crocketed gables.

The church is entered through a vaulted porch blessed with a small Kempe window. The nave is only four bays long, but grand with tall arcades. Here the sandstone is less polluted, although Scott's scraping has left blotchy discoloration. The eastward vista is dominated by the low arches and mighty shafted piers of the crossing. Above the crossing is Scott's bold black-and-red lierne vault, the work of a medievalist with the courage of his convictions. Nantwich has two pulpits, one stone of the 14th century decorated with the most delicate Perpendicular panelling, the other of wood and Jacobean.

The vaulted chancel beyond is of cathedral quality, with lierne ribs and some 70 bosses. How much of this work preceded the Black Death and how much followed it is a puzzle. The east window is a complete work of the later period, while the north and south chancel windows are earlier. We fall back on the old answer to the mid-14th-century conundrum, that 'on-going work was interrupted by the plague'.

The principal adornment of the chancel is its stalls, as fine as those in Chester Cathedral and with a forest of canopies. In the darkness of a spring evening, I watched the shadows move through the pinnacles as through a thicket of cypresses. Shields, crockets and finials crowd above each clerical stall, while misericords beneath record the doings of Nantwich citizens. Here are all the old favourites: a woman beating a man with a spoon, a virgin and unicorn, and a mermaid with a mirror. The reredos was installed in 1919 in a style deferential to the stalls. The sedilia has nodding ogees.

We return to the nave via the transepts. The north is Decorated and holds the church's best window, by Kempe but incorporating medieval glass to form a Tree of Jesse. The other windows are early works by John Hardman. The south transept is Perpendicular, with a monument to Sir Thomas Smith (d.1614), Mayor and

Sheriff of Chester, and his wife. Although the design is conventional, the work is unusually monochromatic, and the better for it. The materials are creamy alabaster and limestone.

The 20th century has been no less active in Nantwich. Across the nave's west end hangs the Jubilee curtain designed by Denise Bates in 1976. In the north aisle is a window of 1985 by Michael Farrar-Bell. It commemorates a local farmer by portraying all Creation in the Cheshire countryside. Its subject is seen peacefully walking his dog through the trees while the inhabitants of Noah's Ark swirl above his head.

Cornwall

Launceston

ST MARY
Carved granite facades, 20th-century woodwork

Launceston is the premier church of Cornwall in the former county capital. The old town clusters round the castle walls like a mini-Windsor. The church lies down a lane from the market square, its carved wall decoration unparalleled in England. Apart from an older tower, the church is the creation of one man, Sir Henry Trecarrel, whose house is now a ruin at Trecarrel five miles to the south. The church was built in 1511–24 in the final burst of patronage that took place shortly before the Reformation. Whether Trecarrel intended to display his wealth or his piety is not known, possibly both. His coat of arms and that of his wife cover the church exterior.

The ornament is what Pevsner calls a 'barbarous profusion'. Not even masons in easy-to-work limestone attempted such ornament elsewhere in England. To chisel solid granite, however crude the result, must have involved a phenomenal effort and heavy expenditure. The carving covers all sides and includes the pinnacles on the buttresses. The motifs, apart from the Trecarrel arms, are quatrefoils, shields, flowers and mottoes. They are repetitive and not especially beautiful, but they are prolific. The work has been attributed to masons from St Mary, Truro, begun in 1504. On the outside of the east wall is a prone figure of Mary Magdalene. A local custom is to throw a stone which, if it rests on her back, will bring good luck. The porch has more complex imagery, including St George and the Dragon and St Martin dividing his cloak, as well as the herbal ingredients of St Mary's ointment.

The interior conforms to the usual Cornish plan. It has eight continuous bays with no division between nave and chancel and no sign of a rood loft or stair. The roof has carved members, tiny angels and apparently over 400 bosses. Launceston has four works of art that merit attention. The Gothic rood screen is by the Rashleigh Pinwills of Plymouth of 1911, and is as fine as anything imported by F. C. Eden or the Seddings from London. The Pinwells were also responsible for the woodwork of the reredos. The pulpit is Perpendicular, painted black but with gold details and a red and green ribbed stem. There is a profusion of foliage in the ogival panels. The bench-ends are, for once, not Tudor but Art Nouveau. Their theme is the Works of the Lord. One near the entrance proclaims, in what might be a theme for all Cornish bench-ends, 'O All Ye Green Things Upon The Earth'.

Against the north wall is that rare object in Cornwall, an accomplished Georgian memorial. This is to two friends, Granville Piper and Richard Wise, both mayors of Launceston. Their own presence is confined to two busts, while prominence is given instead to statues of the Virtues, standing between pairs of superimposed Corinthian columns in an imposing design.

Cumbria

Wreay

ST MARY
Sarah Losh's Lombardic Revival

This is one of the most eccentric small churches in England. The hamlet of Wreay, pronounced ree-ah, sits round a formal green of beeches, firs and cherry trees, and is near Carlisle (another Wreay is by Ullswater). Here stands a church which, but for the severity of its stone, might be on a hillside in northern Italy.

The church was commissioned and designed by a local woman, Sarah Losh, in memory of her sister and parents. Her portrait hangs inside the door. Many visitors have wondered how a provincial lady, even of good education (her father knew Wordsworth), could have acquired such detailed knowledge of Italian Romanesque and Early Christian architecture. There are other 'Lombardic' churches in England, for example at Wilton (Wilts), designed by T. H. Wyatt for the Countess of Pembroke. Wilton was begun in 1841, and Wreay in 1835.

The answer must lie in the talent and education of Miss Losh herself. She was the daughter of an educated ironmaster, John Losh, owner of a Newcastle factory. Sarah and her sister Catherine were taken to Italy in 1817. She knew French, Latin and Greek and when her sister died in 1835, the fifty-year-old Sarah determined to pour into her memorial all she had acquired of art and architecture. We know of no assistant in the venture; the building appears to be entirely her work. The only other inspiration was a Major William Thain, a local hero and soldier, who fought at Waterloo and died on the Afghan frontier in 1842. He sent Sarah a pine cone, her last missive from him before he died. The motif appears everywhere in the church.

The shape is a simple box, with a steep gable on the west front. The round arched openings are decorated with flora and fauna, boldly carved, slightly abstract, and larger than life size. Among other motifs are the caterpillar, chrysalis and butterfly as symbols of life, death and resurrection. On each corner of the side elevations is a monstrous gargoyle.

Inside, the nave is plain, unaisled and outwardly dull, until we examine the details. The clerestory has small arched windows in triplets, containing lovely stained glass. The middle opening uses black glass in which are set brilliantly coloured leaves. The glass in the nave windows is of fragments brought back from the ruined archbishop's palace in Paris by Sarah's cousin, William. The furnishings border on Disneyesque, except that they are stylistically harmonious and superbly executed.

The font is adorned with butterflies and pomegranates and was mostly carved by Losh herself. Pevsner calls it 'Byzantino-Naturalistic'. Stone lilies float in water of glass. Losh's eagle lectern and pelican reading desk rise out of trunks covered in bark. The pulpit is a hollowed-out trunk. The adjacent candle-holder is, I think, a giant thistle. The chancel arch has a frieze of angels and palm trees, a work of great elegance.

The chancel is even more remarkable. It has an arcaded apse with closely spaced columns and painted surrounds. The deep clerestory has windows with metal stencils of fern fossils. All this work appears to be without any academic or aesthetic forerunner. Historians have failed to find any pattern-book (except possibly by a German scholar) from which Losh could have derived her inspiration. We know only that her gardener did much of the wood carving and a local mason, William Hindson, the stonework. It is said that Hindson was treated to a trip to Italy by Losh to improve his technique.

The mausoleum for Catherine and Sarah Losh is in the churchyard and is of stones laid casually in a 'cyclopean' style. Next to it is a good Victorian reproduction of the Bewcastle Cross, which is better than the original in that it is now less eroded. Unlike almost all the works in this book, Wreay appears to have been the creation of a single original mind. Sarah Losh was an individual genius, an architectural Charlotte Brontë. The Arts and Crafts Movement took half a century to catch up with her.

Derbyshire

Ashbourne

ST OSWALD
Cockayne and Boothby tombs,
19th- and 20th-century glass

Ashbourne sits at the southernmost tip of the Peak District and thus of the spine of England. Here we bid farewell to the soft flatlands of the south and head for Dovedale and the harsh Pennine Way. The town has a high street and square largely devoid of 20th-century intrusion. The church, which was to George Eliot 'the finest mere parish church in the kingdom', lies at its western extremity, its spire soaring over a churchyard which, on my last visit, was carpeted with daffodils. A verger assured me there were more than 100 varieties.

The exterior of pink limestone is odd, the cruciform plan somehow out of proportion. There is a long Early Gothic collegiate chancel and massive 212-ft crossing tower and spire. There are wide eastern aisles to the transepts. Yet the nave is hardly worth the name, short with a single aisle to the south. Ashbourne church was for clergy and gentry, but apparently not for locals. Small wonder the Methodists were so popular in these parts. Yet the building contains some of Derbyshire's finest monuments and its best stained glass. It is possible that parts of the spire and nave aisle were by a local mason, Henry Yevele, who left Ashbourne for London in the mid 14th century, to become the master architect of English Perpendicular and builder of Westminster Hall.

The interior is as eccentric as the exterior. No corner is without interest: carved kings and queens, bell ropes, Green Men, a lush chancel roof of 1963 by S. E. Dykes Bower and a reredos with scenes from Dovedale. A window in the north transept has even been set at an angle to catch the rays of the evening sun. Here is a church with grand and intimate spaces, a church of something for everyone.

Pride of place goes to the Cockayne Chapel in the east aisle of the north transept which is filled with their tombs. John Cockayne was steward to John of Gaunt, whose wife, Blanche, was daughter of the local Earl of Derby. Cockaynes were active in national politics throughout the Wars of the Roses and into the Tudor period. They remained powers in the district, at Ashbourne Hall, until the 1670s when debts forced a sale to the Boothby family. The tombs range from the early 15th to the late 16th centuries and include brasses, chests, incised slabs and wall memorials. The finest medieval work, to Sir John Cockayne (d.1447) and his wife, is of Derbyshire alabaster, he in armour, she in a magnificent medieval costume, with angel weepers holding shields round the chest. Near them are buried two centuries of Cockaynes, a mortuary of ages, a gathering of the clan, so common in England yet without equal elsewhere in Europe, and symbol of continuity and stability in local land tenure.

At the southern end of the group is a gem, Thomas Banks's figure of Penelope Boothby, who died aged five in 1791. The child lies as if asleep within her marble effigy. Her figure is visible under her gown with unashamed poignancy, her little toe gingerly covered. The sash of velvet is chiselled to a different texture from the cloth of the dress. Queen Charlotte was said to have broken into tears on seeing the statue at a Royal Academy exhibition. Evincing such a reaction was regarded as a challenge to late-Georgian sculpture.

After the tombs, the windows. If these great churches must be rendered gloomy by Victorian glass let it be the best. Ashbourne's glass is excellent. The east and west windows are by Kempe, the latter a Tree of Jesse, its figures in perpetual Kempeian motion. Another Kempe is in the north wall, with his wheatsheaf signature. In the south aisle is a 1904 work by Christopher Whall, commemorating a wife and daughter who died in a local fire. This is Arts and Crafts at its most ethereal. Girls play the organ dressed in medieval clothes with flowers and crowns in their hair, the celestial city visible through a thicket of thorns. Whall's signature was his own thumbprint, seen in the clearer panes. In the west wall of the south transept is a work of 1933 by the Bromsgrove Guild, brilliantly coloured but hard to see. Ashbourne church is one of the finest works of art in the county, and should rank alongside the magnificent historic mansions.

Devon

Cullompton

ST ANDREW
Carved screen, Perpendicular roof, aisle fan vault

There is nothing complex to Cullompton. It is a monument to English Perpendicular Gothic, as straightforward as its neighbour, Ottery St Mary, is confused. The tower, roof, screen and Lane Chapel are well preserved. The restorer's decision to reinstate bright colours to the wood surfaces, offset by white walls and pale stone dressings, is admirable.

The church sits away from the centre of the town, down its own lane. The tower is later than the rest of the church, dated 1545–9, with Ham stone dressings on a sandstone structure. It is highly decorated, with small pinnacles and gargoyles sitting on the tops of two buttresses. The exterior is most remarkable for the ostentatious Lane Chapel attached to the south side of the church c.1526–9. The buttresses have the patron's shears and ships, and many depictions of JL (John Lane). The rival Moore Chapel on the north-east side of the church is a more modest affair.

The first impression of the interior, approached from the west under the tower, is superb. The nave is prefaced by a low gallery of 1637, set on charming Ionic columns, with evangelists between blind arches. This increases the drama of Cullompton's famous roof and screen. The roof is wagon shaped but with the panels and cross-braces that are normally features of a flat roof. They are richly worked, rising from angel posts. The chancel divide is marked only by a carved rood beam with a coat of arms. The colours throughout are blue, red and gold, renewed in the chancel but not in the nave. These roofs would do credit to a Tudor banqueting hall. The pattern is repeated in the aisles.

The Cullompton screen is remarkable for its complete-ness and the purity of its decoration, despite frequent renewal. The colouring is unashamedly fresh, with blues, reds, greens and gold detailing. The coving projects in a series of fans and the original cornice has vine leaves and other foliage, all still crisp. The church possesses the remains of the old rood Golgotha, a stark mass of rocks, skulls and bones. Now at the back of the south aisle, it would have formed the base for the Crucifix above the rood loft. Why not restore it?

The chancel is divided from the side chapels by further screens. These reflect the rivalry between the local Moore and Lane families. The Moores of Moorehays House were traditional landed wealth, John Lane an *arriviste* cloth merchant. The screen to the Moore Chapel is in a flat Perpendicular, crowned by angels holding Moore family shields. The roof bosses are particularly splendid. Lane's response was to construct a completely new south aisle, with fan vaulting of a lavishness rare in a parish church. The guide suggests that a wooden roof was replaced by a stone one specifically to compete with the

Moores. Or perhaps Lane saw the new Dorset aisle at Ottery St Mary, built at the same time *c*.1520. Either way, expense can have been no object. There are carved saints and angels everywhere, even filling the buttress panels and vault pendants. The whole chamber shimmers with sunlight and forms a splendid climax to the interior. A rare West Country Burne-Jones window is an added delight.

The extraordinary preservation of Cullompton is due to William Froude, Brunel's engineer on the local section of the Great Western Railway. He lived in the town in the 1840s and paid for the restoration and recolouring of the chancel. He left the nave roof, to which he felt the parishioners should contribute. They declined, their meanness evident to this day. The tower holds a complete set of ten bells. These can be seen in the course of a climb up to the tower roof, from where there is a view out over the soft Devon hills.

Ottery St Mary

Miniature Exeter Cathedral, painted roof, fan-vaulted aisle

Ottery St Mary sits cosily in its nest on the banks of the River Otter. At first sight it might be a French monastery that came to Devon on a visit, fell in love with the place and decided to stay. Twin towers, high gables and triple lancet windows are those of a Norman collegiate foundation. But closer inspection indicates a thoroughly English church, combining dash with domesticity. The stone is honey-coloured, fertilising colonies of lichen. Nothing is lacking.

The church's origins were indeed French, the patrons being secular canons from Rouen. The present structure owes its appearance to Bishop Grandison of Exeter, who wrested the church from Rouen in 1335 and two years later founded a college of forty members at Ottery. Grandison commenced rebuilding in 1342, using the new cathedral at Exeter as a model. He erected a 'posh' east end, two bays larger than the west end, lengthened even further by a Lady Chapel, and furnished with a second pair of transepts.

Also unusual are the two towers over the main transepts, features otherwise found only at Exeter. One tower has a spire with a medieval weathercock fitted with tubes to 'whistle' in the wind, now defunct. Equally distinctive is the absence of 14th-century tracery. The windows of many lights within a single arch are Early Gothic in style, a form of 'classical' Gothic sometimes used by senior prelates at this time.

The interior of Ottery offers connoisseurs a test of taste. The church received the attention of successive Victorians, including Edward Blore and William Butterfield, but their restoration was overlaid in 1977 by vigorous and controversial repainting. The colouring of the roofs, vaults and screens, though not the carved stone, is startling and distracting. Yet as at Cullompton, the intention was to reinstate the visual impact of a medieval church, however upsetting to the modern eye. I found Ottery's colours grew on me. The Lady Chapel, restored by the Victorian Henry Woodyer and now a century old, is visually subdued in comparison.

The view east from the nave extends through the

crossing and into the chancel. The arcades are plain but nave and aisle roofs are bright with white, red and blue paint, adorned with magnificent bosses. The crossing vault has bosses worthy of their Exeter inspiration. The boss depicting Grandison himself is at the centre. The vault of the chancel, the visual climax to the view from the nave, is curvilinear. Here the motif is a four-petalled rosette, the ribs serving simply as decoration. Pevsner attributes this work to William Joy of Wells. The carvers of the Ottery bosses are from Exeter, of unsurpassed excellence. In the nave arcades are two magnificent Decorated tombs, of Bishop Grandison's brother, Sir Otho (d.1359), and his wife Beatrix (d.1374). The canopies are both giant ogees, decorated with no fewer than 50 shields for their coats of arms. I am surprised nobody had the courage to paint these.

We now enter the Dorset aisle, running parallel to the north aisle and the only substantial addition to the old church. This is a magnificent work, built in the early 16th century. The arcading is luxuriant, with capitals formed of scrolls, vine leaves and corbel heads portraying an owl, a Green Man and even an elephant. The aisle is most remarkable for its fan vault, with curious openwork pendants, some of them twisted. The west window is a fierce Victorian work by Wailes, best seen against the setting sun.

The south transept is a contrast. Its mosaic wall tiles are by Butterfield and were installed by the Coleridge family. The vicar of Ottery at the end of the 18th century was the poet's father. The serene late-Victorian memorial is to a Lady Coleridge (d.1878). The great clock is believed to be Grandison's original, with one of the oldest mechanisms extant. The outer rim has 24 hours, not 12.

The chancel is dominated by the great stone reredos. The basic structure is 14th century, but it was extensively wrecked in the Reformation. The architectural sculpture was replaced by the Victorians and the figures were contributed by Herbert Read in the 1930s. Again, modern colour is dominant. The sedilia is superb, lofty and richly crocketed.

The cathedral plan continues east of the reredos, though with almost toylike smallness. Here is an ambulatory, a stone screen and loft and finally a Lady Chapel. This has an east window with no fewer than eight lights. There are corbels carved with the heads of Grandison and his sister, and bosses with scenes from the life of the Virgin. Much of the woodwork is original, including oak stalls and a wooden eagle lectern, one of the earliest in the country.

Dorset

Christchurch

PRIORY
Norman exterior, Decorated screen,
Perpendicular tombs and chantries

Of all the great churches of England, Christchurch is
probably the least well known. Its tower rises beyond
the water meadows of the River Avon near the coast,
which has taken more punishment from planners than
any. The continuous ribbon of retirement suburbs from
Lymington to Poole is a landscape without redemption.
I prefer the desolate mills and blasted tips of the north
of England to this endless drabness. Christchurch Priory
is like Gulliver awakening from a long sleep on the
shore and now struggling to escape the bonds of modern
life.

The church is sensational. The view of the reredos
as climax to the Norman nave and crossing arch is a
coup de théâtre of church architecture. The sanctuary
is adorned with Gothic treasures, culminating in the
Salisbury Chantry. Christchurch, like Sherborne and
Beverley Minster (Yorks, ER), has the proportions of a
cathedral, being transferred from priory to parish church
at the Reformation. Little damage was done at the time,
except to the monastic buildings. The church survived

virtually intact and even Benjamin Ferrey's Victorian restoration seems unobtrusive.

The sequence of tower, nave, chancel and Lady Chapel forms the longest parish church in England. The central tower fell in the 15th century and was replaced by the present west tower. The Norman nave and transepts survive, the former with Early Gothic windows. They convey enormous strength, alleviated by the north transept's sumptuous blind arcading. This north transept is one of the most spectacular works of Norman design in England, despite the reckless intrusion of a Perpendicular window. The stair turret is most celebrated, a series of graceful arcading on the ground floor, colonettes on the second, a bold trellis pattern on the third and then more blind arcading at the top. Could anyone pull off such a composition today?

Continuing round the exterior, we suddenly meet Perpendicular for the rebuilt chancel and Lady Chapel. The former has four-light clerestory windows, the latter a most unusual upper storey. This was used as a grammar school and is now a museum.

The church is entered through the north porch. This is no mere parish shelter, but a ceremonial meeting place for the prior and the burgesses of the town. It is in the richest Early Gothic style, with the double doorway into the church flanked each side by no fewer than six Purbeck shafts. The tierceron vault and effusive bosses are Victorian restorations in the Decorated mode. The interior is an essay in contrasts. The Norman nave is massive. The aisle and clerestory windows are Early Gothic insertions and the wooden roof is Victorian reproduction.

But the great vista eastwards dominates the scene. This is modulated first by the dark height of the old crossing, the earliest part of the church, then by the chancel, a blaze of light crowned by a lierne vault.

Glimpsed over the crossing pulpitum is the enormous 14th-century stone reredos, a masterpiece of English Decorated carving. It depicts a Tree of Jesse surmounted by a crowded Epiphany. The composition is full of movement and vigour. The remaining niches need filling, the more so since the composition is itself surmounted by a 1967 mural of Christ the Saviour by Hans Feibusch. If murals can be so confidently replaced, why not statuary?

This reredos must have been re-erected when the new Perpendicular chancel was built almost two centuries later. At its heart is the Great Quire, filled with some of the finest stalls and misericords in the region. The latter include such favourites as a fox in a pulpit preaching to a flock of geese. High above the stalls, the shafts end in foliated capitals that have been painted and gilded, recreating the richness of the Perpendicular originals.

A different eastwards view is down the south aisle towards the chancel. This is framed by a slender lancet, erupting in a complex lierne vault. The aisle is lined with memorials and two chantry chapels, to Robert Harys (in 1525) and John Draper (prior in 1520). These date from the last burst of Perpendicular before the Reformation, Draper's chantry already showing Renaissance motifs. He was the prior who had to surrender the foundation's wealth to Henry VIII, but was allowed a pension of £133 a year and a comfortable home. Perhaps it is to his diplomacy that Christchurch owes its survival.

The north aisle chantries are richer still. The master-piece, the Salisbury Chantry, was built in 1529 for Margaret Pole, Countess of Salisbury and owner of the manor of Christchurch. She was to be executed by Henry VIII for the outspoken Catholic views of her son, then studying in Rome. She claimed Plantagenet title to the throne as daughter of the Duke of Clarence. The chantry's fan vaulting, canopied niches, tracery and panelling are worthy of her.

The Lady Chapel stands out to the east of the ambulatory, its wall arcading and reredos of the utmost richness. The priest's doors in the north wall and the stops to the lierne vault overhead are elaborately decorated. The church retains three Saxon crypts.

Milton Abbey

Decorated crossing and windows, Pugin glass

The abbey church was an ancient Benedictine foundation burnt in 1309 but not rebuilt beyond its crossing. It owes its picturesque setting to the Earl of Dorchester's decision in 1771 to demolish the old abbey buildings and erect a new house on the site. He moved the village to a valley a mile away. The village street once stretched south and east of the abbey, where there is now a school cricket field and golf course. The sweep of the church, William Chambers' house and Capability Brown's grounds, set in a glade amid wooded slopes, is one of the great set pieces of English landscape.

The abbey church still belongs to the diocese. It is built of warm Ham stone, Chilmark stone and flint and consists only of an aisled chancel and crossing with tower and transepts. It is thus a 14th-century fragment of what was intended to be a massive structure. Blind arcades to the east indicate a vanished Lady Chapel while the west front has springers for nave arcades that were never built. What stands is reminiscent of a college chapel, serene in the height and uniformity of its elevation and with magnificent transept windows.

These windows dominate our first impression of the interior, since we enter directly into what was meant to be the crossing. Most of the work is Decorated Gothic of the mid 14th century. The sensational south window has seven lights below a screen of Reticulated tracery, four tiers of cusped lozenges, like a giant net hung down from the gable. The glass is a Tree of Jesse by A. W. N. Pugin. The later north transept window is no less spectacular but here the Perpendicular style has taken over. The east and west windows of the transepts are astonishingly high, Perpendicular engineering at its most spectacular. The lierne vault becomes a fan under the tower. The walls, in contrast to the sophistication of the fenestration, are strangely roughcast, of stone, Purbeck marble and flint. This whole space is one of the glories of English Gothic.

In the north transept stands the monument to the couple who destroyed the original village but perhaps saved the church, Joseph Damer, later Earl of Dorchester, and his wife. The tomb was designed by Robert Adam, the effigies carved by Agostino Carlini. They portray a husband gazing down lovingly on his dead spouse, both lying comfortably on a bed. Next door stands an unusual

Art Nouveau font by J. A. Jerichau. Two large angels dominate the composition; the water bowl is hardly noticeable at their feet.

The chancel is divided from the crossing by a restored pulpitum screen which carries the organ. On its east side are two panel paintings dating from the 15th century, of the founder of the monastery, King Athelstan, and his mother Egwynna. The choir culminates in a vast Perpendicular reredos, restored in plaster by James Wyatt in the 18th century. This is painfully lacking in statuary, surely a fit project for a modern benefactor. High on the north wall is a rare medieval tabernacle of carved wood. This would once have hung before the reredos to house the Sacrament.

In the south aisle is a memorial to a member of the Tregonwell family, who acquired the abbey after the Dissolution and before its sale to the Damers. John Tregonwell bequeathed his library to the church in thanks for being saved when he fell from its roof as a child. His pantaloons allegedly filled with air and broke his fall. I assume that this was the first successful parachute.

Sherborne

ABBEY OF ST MARY
Complete fan vault, carved bosses, misericords

Sherborne, like Beverley, Selby and Tewkesbury, requires a disclaimer. Prior to the Reformation it ranked with the great monastic churches that are now cathedrals. Indeed it was a cathedral until 1075 and a monastery church until the Dissolution. Since then, like most former monastic foundations, it has been parochial. The town was fortunate in what it inherited and has been careful in conserving that fortune. The abbey lies in the centre of the town, surrounded by ancient buildings. Abbey and town are both of Ham stone, a glorious material warmer than even the most creamy Cotswold. The church thus sits well in context, its size lightened by windows of the Perpendicular style at its gayest and most confident.

Sherborne's Saxon–Norman origins explain the heavy central tower and the asymmetry of the first bay of the nave arcade. The porch is Norman, as are the main crossing transepts. The 13th century added the Early Gothic Lady Chapel with Purbeck shafts and stiff-leaf capitals, and Bishop Roger's Chapel off the north choir aisle. Key to the abbey's character is the transformation of the remaining core by its abbots in the 15th century. The cause was a revolt by the local citizens against the abbot in 1437, during which the nave roof and tower were burnt. For this the town was punished by being compelled to pay for the reconstruction, and pay for the best. It took the abbot half a century to complete the task.

His monks did not enjoy the finished work for long. Just seventeen of them were left to surrender Sherborne to the king on its dissolution in 1539. The new church was purchased and then sold to the townspeople by a local magnate, Sir John Horsey. The abbey on which they had had to spend so much money duly became their church. They understandably respected it. Only a westward extension, which had been the parish's church of All Hallows, was demolished. The eastern chapels were converted for the use of Sherborne School, remaining so until restored to the main church in the 1930s.

The interior is uniformly Perpendicular, with the exceptions noted above. Both nave and choir have immense panelled piers, those in the choir continuing uninterrupted up to the vaults. Sherborne has some of the finest fan vaults in England. They cover virtually the whole interior, except for the nave vaults which have liernes, and the south transept, which is not vaulted. There is evidence that the design existed even before the fire of 1437, making it the first high fan in England. The nave vault, built at the end of the century, is sufficiently similar to suggest the same hand or at least the same design. John Harvey comments that the work 'is very distinctive and must be the creation of a great master; it is quite possible that his name is known, but unconnected with any existing work through which the authorship of Sherborne could be traced'. Harvey's best guess is William Smyth, who was working at Wells in the second half of the 15th century.

The essence of the Sherborne fans is that, unlike the more decorative fans of Gloucester, Bath or Cambridge, they do not overlap and thus cut each other off. Nor do they have pendants or other foibles. The components are structural. Each fan is a complete semicircle (in fact a polygon). Individual ribs leap from the fan to cross the central vault, intersecting in a series of lozenges. This gives to the starburst of the fan the tautness of earlier lierne ribs. The choir vault is narrower than that of the nave: its diagonal ribs buckle and twist and the fans come closer to touching, like exotic palm trees. The vault in the north transept, different again, might be that of a bedchamber, all frills and lace.

The vault intersections are punctuated with bosses. They are masterpieces of medieval carving, easier to study in the guide than with the naked eye. Most represent the dominant themes of late 15th-century Sherborne, the red and white roses of the civil war, the abbot's rebus, the coat of arms of Henry VII. They also portray simple scenes of domestic life and legend. Dogs chew on a bone. A pelican 'in her piety' plucks blood from her breast to feed her young. An owl is mobbed by birds. In the south transept the corbels, more crudely carved, are of men and women in the fashions of the period. There are a number of Green Men with foliage issuing from their mouths. The well-known boss of the mermaid holding a mirror and comb is high in the eastern bay of the nave. This is sophisticated and enlightened decoration. I would pit Sherborne's roof against any contemporary work of the Italian Renaissance.

More medieval carving is to be found in the choir. Ten misericords survive under the Victorian stalls, including the well-known woman beating her husband and master beating a boy. In the latter case the carver even portrays the weals in the boy's bottom. The pupils all have faces of monkeys. One of the bench-ends has a poignant old man selling cherries. After this vitality, Sherborne's extensive memorial sculpture can seem stilted. In the Wykeham Chapel is the monument to Sir John Horsey and his son, purchaser of the abbey at the time of the Dissolution. He died in 1546, when knights were still portrayed in armour but forms were appearing in Renaissance tomb canopies.

Forty years later and across in St Katherine's Chapel, John Leweston was commemorated in Elizabethan classicism, though still recumbent and in prayer. A century later, memorial art had changed again. The south transept contains the standing monument to John Digby (d.1698), grand, pompous, splendid and very much alive. His calf is well turned, his wig is in place and his adoring wives are on either side. Beneath is his eulogy: 'He was naturally inclined to avoid the hurry of a publick life, yet careful to keep up to the port of his quality, was willing to be at ease, but scorned obscurity.' Beside the supporting columns are two putti weeping stone tears, whether of mirth or sadness is not clear.

The present Chapel of St Mary le Bow was the head-master's drawing-room and study of Sherborne School. The old fireplace can still be seen in the east wall. Next door in the Lady Chapel is a lovely engraved glass reredos by Laurence Whistler of 1968.

Wimborne Minster

ST CUTHBURGA
Moses carving, Uvedale monument

The old minster sits in the centre of this market town like a mini-cathedral, much loved and much visited. Even the stand on which the churchyard sign is mounted is a work of art. The exterior looks eccentric, with two towers, one Norman at the crossing and another Perpendicular at the west. The stone is odder still, Dorset limestone interspersed with what Clifton-Taylor calls a 'dark rust-brown conglomerate of the Tertiary period', dug from the heaths north of the New Forest. The effect, seen also at Ellingham (Hants) and Bere Regis, is of a quilt of coloured rags. It is not unpleasing, but detracts from the vertical line of the Gothic building. If the desire was for economy, the brown stone presumably being cheaper, it is odd that the masons did not concentrate this stone rather than disperse it at random.

Inside are all the components of an English church: Norman core, Early Gothic east end, Decorated aisles and adornments and Perpendicular 'topping and tailing'. Wimborne was a Saxon nunnery wrecked by the Danes but revived as a college of canons by Edward the Confessor. The Norman nave and crossing are powerful, Saxon in plan. The nave arcades are late Norman, with zigzag arches and carved heads peering out of the mouldings. The clerestory is Perpendicular.

At the west end behind the tower screen is a fine Norman font resting on Purbeck marble shafts, with a Victorian font cover. High on the wall is an astronomical clock, its mechanism dating from the early 14th century with the earth at the centre of the universe. It is not linked with the 'Quarter Jack' on the tower outside, where a model soldier strikes each 15 minutes. Erected in 1612, he was originally a monk, but became a patriotic Grenadier during the Napoleonic wars.

We pass east through the two crossing arches to the chancel, where three large Early Gothic windows rise the full height of the east wall. The lancets are barely pointed, with black Purbeck marble shafts. From the nave, they make a perfect foil for the Norman arches. The stained glass is Flemish 16th century, compatible with Early Gothic windows. The central window was given by the Bankes family of Kingston Lacy, and represents the Tree of Jesse.

In the north chancel aisle stands the superb Jacobean monument to Sir Edmund Uvedale (d.1606). It is unusually restrained, the effigy lying head on hand, staring into the future while garlands and ribbonwork play round the inscription above. For some reason he has two left feet. Near him is a Saxon oak chest hewn out of a solid trunk of undressed wood, a superb survivor. On the south side of the chancel lies the tomb of John Beaufort, Duke of Somerset (d.1444) and his wife, grandparents of Henry VII. Alabaster effigies are set on a chest of Purbeck marble, portrayed solemnly holding hands. Next to them is Wimborne's famous Moses corbel, dating from the late 12th century and therefore earlier than the arch in which it is set. The head has flowing hair and plaited beard.

In the south chapel is another Wimborne curiosity, the Ettricke tomb. The chest is of a local lawyer who, in a temper, said he would not be buried inside or outside the church of his native town. He contrived eventually to be buried in the wall. Convinced he was dying in 1693 he even had the date inscribed on his tomb. It had to be changed when he survived another ten years, the masons not trying too hard to erase the former date. In the sanctuary wall is a small brass put up in the 15th century to King Ethelred the Unready, defender against the

Danes and buried in the old convent on the site. This is the only royal brass known in England. Wimborne has a fine chained library.

Essex

Copford

ST MICHAEL
12th-century wall paintings

The sumptuousness of Copford is explained by the presence of Copford Hall, ancient manor of the Bishops of London. Its great cedars offer a splendid backdrop to the approach to the church from the road. Even they are scant preparation for the interior. Copford's Norman wall paintings are among the best in England, ranking with those of Ickleton (Cambs) and Kempley (Gloucs).

Copford is a 12th-century church, heavily restored. The inside is at first sight odd. The nave walls have three springers of a lost tunnel vault, rare in a parish church. The removal of the vault was probably to avert a collapse, since the roof is clearly 15th century. The south arcade appears to be mainly late 13th century, but its arches are so varied that it is hard to believe they are of the same date. The eastern one appears Transitional Norman, the middle one looks late 13th century and is partly of brick. If so, this is among the earliest medieval brick in England, some of it possibly reused Roman brick.

Paintings cover almost all the wall surfaces. As at Kempley they were applied to wet plaster, and were thus

34

more robust than later medieval works. Nonetheless, all have been restored with varying degrees of vehemence after their discovery in the 19th century under layers of Reformation whitewash. Those in the apse were over-painted by Daniel Bell in the 1870s. It is known that he added a number of details of his own, including a crown on Christ's head. The Annunciation above the chancel arch is a completely Victorian work. All have recently been restored 'as found', with overpainting left in place.

The details of the paintings are covered in the guide. Those in the chancel are the familiar Byzantine/Roman-esque characters of the saints and apostles surrounding Christ in Majesty. Here Bell's decorative flourishes can seem intrusive, especially round the windows, which are filled with fierce Victorian glass. The underside of the chancel arch carries the signs of the zodiac, as a link between the Earthly and Heavenly realms. The Copford masterpiece is in the nave above the pulpit, a rare example of the Raising of Jairus's Daughter, clearly still in its 12th-century form. This story was often taken as a metaphor of the Resurrection, with the father pleading with Christ, who gazes into the distance. Much of the nave painting is abstract, almost Art Deco.

A huge wooden frame supports the bell loft at the west end of the nave. The original Perpendicular screen survives and the Victorian pulpit includes a charming St Michael on its newel post. On the floor are original tiles and, in the chancel, mosaics. I am told that those by the pulpit were designed by women from Abingdon prison.

Thaxted

ST JOHN
Flying-buttressed spire, Perpendicular windows,
Adam and Eve glass

The town of Thaxted is queen of Essex and her crown is the church. The steeple stands out over the surrounding fields. The town streets all seem to bend in its direction over ancient cobbles and past timber-framed houses. This was a place of thatchers, hence its name, then of cutlers, hence the name of its town hall, and finally of cloth, to which the church owes its richness. Thaxted is a corrective to those who find East Anglian Perpendicular monotonous. We do not know who built this church, but we do know of the remarkable vicars, Conrad Noel and Jack Putterill, who for most of the 20th century made it a centre of Anglo-Catholic evangelism. Gustav Holst came to live in Thaxted and played the organ. The town's name was given to the tune from *The Planets*, later used for 'I Vow to Thee, My Country'.

The tower is almost as high as the church is long, perfectly proportioned from base to spire. This latter is supported by flying buttresses and has ribs with crockets. The side walls of the chancel and aisles are filled with beautiful windows, those in the chancel having straight tops, entirely filling the walls with glass. Ferocious gargoyles abound. The porches are richly decorated, the north one especially so. The south porch has unusual entrances in all three sides and a star vault. Both porches have upstairs rooms. The room above the north porch is a private chapel dedicated to John Ball, 'priest-martyr' and organiser of the 1381 Peasants' Revolt.

The interior is saved from blandness by its proportions and by the ingenuity with which the transepts throw shadows across the central space. The plan dates from *c*.1340, leaving a late Decorated nave with beautifully rhythmic arcades. From this core the Perpendicular architecture seems to blossom outwards. The nave aisles are wider than the nave, while the transepts are so short as almost to be 'false'. The chancel has aisles of its own, only slightly narrower than those in the nave, with arcades with charming pierced spandrels. Above soar Thaxted's clerestories, and roofs of Tudor oak.

The church is a gallery of medieval stone carving. Grotesques, monsters, bishops, saints adorn the rafters in happy congregation. Carving in the north transept is truly astonishing. Nodding ogee arcading is infested with angels, popping out of every nook, smiling and playing instruments. Conrad Noel filled the empty niches and dressed every altar. Gaudy banners hang in the chancel, restoring some of the colour of the pre-Reformation church. In the south transept is a lovely 14th-century German Madonna.

The glass is mostly clear throughout. As a result, when I visited on an early spring day, the windows were filled with the sight of cherry blossom. This perfectly matched the flowers of the Garden of Eden, depicted in the lovely medieval window (*c*.1450) of Adam and Eve in the south aisle.

Gloucestershire

Chipping Campden

ST JAMES
Cotswold tower, clothiers' tombs, altar hangings

Chipping Campden rivalled Cirencester, Northleach and Chipping Norton (Oxon) as capital of the 15th-century Cotswold wool trade. A dozen of its merchants rose to become lord mayors of London. They put a sheep on top of the Royal Exchange and a Woolsack under the Chancellor. Chipping is a corruption of cheaping, or market place, and the town's status derived both from the sheep downs and from its place on the wool route over the Cotswolds from the Welsh Marches. Prosperity seems to have been unaffected by the Hundred Years War and enhanced by the Wars of the Roses. Not until the rise of cloth manufacture in the valleys were these hill communities challenged.

The wealth is still displayed in the procession of houses along the high street, and in the almshouses and domed gatehouse to the old manor near the church. Campden was lucky in its 20th-century preservation, and is rightly celebrated as a Cotswold town that has settled gracefully for village status in its old age. Today the church tower rises above a bridge of twelve apostle lime trees and an arboretum of evergreens. Its massive outline is softened by thin pilasters strips rising the full height of each face. With pinnacles topping the diagonal buttresses and a pierced parapet with ogee arches, the composition soars over the landscape, an outstanding symbol of England's medieval wealth.

The nave was built from 1488 and is similar to that at Northleach. Concave-sided octagonal piers rise to shallow arches and wide clerestory windows. Over the chancel arch is another large window to light the rood, known as a Cotswold window. The detail is simple, compared for instance with the multiple shafting of the nave at St Mary Redcliffe, Bristol. The impact of Chipping Campden is not decorative but spatial, deriving from the proportion of height to length, the grandeur of the clerestory, and the harmony between arcades, chancel arch and tower arch.

The church is well endowed with monuments to its many benefactors. The largest brass in Gloucestershire lies directly before the altar, eight feet tall. It depicts William Grevel (d.1401), 'formerly a citizen of London and flower of the wool merchants of all England'. Having retired to Gloucestershire after a career in the City (how little changes!), he died before the building of the present church. He lies with his wife Marion in an attitude of prayer. On the north wall of the chancel is a Renaissance tomb of Thomas Smythe (d.1593), complete with two wives and thirteen children. With pediments and strap-work cartouches, it is modelled on George Lloyd's tomb at Ampney Crucis.

Smythe's sons sold the manor in 1610 to Sir Baptist Hicks, another wealthy London merchant. Hicks donated the pulpit, eagle lectern and chancel roof. The church gave him the south chapel for his family tombs. His own tomb is a grand twelve-poster, of black-and-white marble, attributed to Nicholas Stone. It shows Hicks (d.1629), by then Lord Campden, in state robes with his wife. The portrayal of both in old age looks realistic. The other principal monument is to his successor, Lord Campden, and his wife, by Joshua Marshall. It is in sharp contrast to the confidence of the earlier work. This Campden died in the Civil War and stands with his wife, shrouded in their tombs, awaiting the call to Heaven.

Beneath the tower can be seen what is claimed to be England's only complete set of medieval altar hangings, dating from the late 15th century. Faded and restored, they are precious survivals of what must once have been a common possession of every English church, even poor ones.

Cirencester

ST JOHN THE BAPTIST
Perpendicular porch, fan vaults, merchants' tombs

Cirencester is the cathedral of 'woolgothic'. It is not just a masterpiece of Perpendicular art, but a town church whose history can be read and enjoyed with ease. In the 14th and 15th centuries, upland wool was the oil and coal of England. The wealth of the merchant houses of London was built on its trade and the wool towns of Gloucestershire, Yorkshire and East Anglia were its Manchesters and Birminghams. Here the new rich of

England formed their guilds and built and endowed their chantries.

Cirencester, as its name implies, was a Roman centre at the junction of Fosse Way and Ermine Street. Remains of what appears to be the longest Saxon church in England have been uncovered in the abbey grounds next door. The present church was founded in the 12th century, but only the eccentric ground plan reflects this early structure. The chancel survives from the 13th and 14th centuries. Rebuilding began at the start of the 15th century and was still underway a hundred years later.

The church was a joint work of the town and abbey. The abbey owned the wool market and taxed its produce. The abbot was frequently in conflict with the increasingly wealthy merchants, represented by their guilds. The guilds paid for the church tower and new nave, and filled the latter with glass. The tower is the least successful part of the composition, despite its handsome profile over the rooftops of the old town. It does not soar – a planned spire was not added as the walls were considered too weak – but sits on a heavy lower stage, with giant buttresses supporting its east side. The best view is from the east, where the upper storeys sit above the undulating gables and pinnacles of the chapels and aisles like a barque in a heavy sea.

Cirencester is most celebrated for its south porch. This was built by the abbey in 1490, presumably to appease or at least accommodate the merchants in the market. Such medieval porches were of great local importance, for here the conduct of both church and secular business took place. Cirencester's is the largest and most complex in England. It is exceptionally grand, three bays wide, three deep and three storeys tall, though the top storey was rebuilt in the 1830s. The guilds occupied the first and second storeys. It might qualify as England's first office block. The exterior is in the most elaborate Perpendicular Gothic; restless tracery pushes up through panels and oriel windows towards the parapet. Nothing is still.

Cirencester's nave was rebuilt in 1516–30 with soaring Perpendicular arcades and a seven-light Cotswold window above the chancel arch. This is overseen by the arms of Henry VIII. A modern opera house merely lists its patrons by name: a wool church does so with angels carrying their coats of arms high above the nave. Everywhere are the devices and arms of the leading families of the town, the Garstangs, Rychards and Tappers. Opening off the nave are chantry chapels established by individual benefactors *c.*1430–60. At the east end of the south aisle is the Garstang Chapel, erected within the church and surrounded by a fine mid-15th-century wooden screen. Its mullions are carved with the Garstang arms and trademarks in an alternating sequence. The family came from the north, as did many Cotswold merchants. Social mobility did not begin with the Victorians. Henry Garstang's tomb is dated 1464.

The second chantry chapel is a large, four-bay structure built onto the north aisle. It was financed by two courtiers to Richard of York, Richard Dixton and William Prelatte. Both were members of the Weavers' Guild of the Holy Trinity, after which the chapel is named. It is divided from the north aisle by a stone screen and crowned by a fine timber roof. Brasses to the two founders survive, with Prelatte flanked by his two wives. The two aisles north of the chancel were rebuilt *c.*1450, and a chantry established shortly after, its cheerful fan vault financed by the abbey in 1508. It had provided a similar fan in the south porch slightly earlier. This was followed by a new rood screen in the 1520s. Such commissions were the final burst of abbey patronage before the Dissolution.

Cirencester's stained glass was reputedly the equal of Fairford's. It survived the Reformation and even the Civil War, but fell victim to decay. What remained in the late 18th century was gathered together in the main east and west windows. Further fragments survived into the 19th century but were thrown into a railway ditch. Some of these fragments were recovered and reinstated in the south chancel, in a window above the sedilia.

Deerhurst

ST MARY
Saxon fragments, angel sculpture

Deerhurst's church, a former Anglo-Saxon monastery, and the adjacent Odda's Chapel form a picturesque group on the bank of the Severn. Here the Saxons would have sailed up river to found a mission, before pushing on to Tewkesbury and Worcester. Odda's Chapel, founded in 1056, is up a lane a hundred yards to the south and, now disused, is in the care of English Heritage. The church is still functioning, a museum of styles and treasures from almost every period of English architecture, especially Anglo-Saxon. Deerhurst is a delight to the detective.

The approach, past the farmhouse lawn, is deceptive. We see a Perpendicular clerestory above a long row of Tudor aisle windows. However, a closer look reveals earlier work. In the south-east corner is the herringbone pattern of a Saxon wall above a blocked doorway leading from the church to the old cloister. There is more herringbone in the clerestory, and in the tower which is virtually all Saxon work. Nothing seems to have been demolished, merely patched by each generation like a pauper's garment.

The interior of Deerhurst has been much restored. The limewashed walls look new and white, the archaeological fragments obviously left as curios. It is an exceptional survival, the Saxon work evident in the tall narrow nave and the west and east walls. The west wall is entirely Anglo-Saxon, with openings at three levels. At the top level are two windows with the triangular heads characteristic of Saxon work. The east wall retains the Saxon chancel arch. There are some 30 Saxon doorways and other openings at Deerhurst. The Early Gothic arcades have a superb collection of capitals, from stiff-leaf to arabesque. A man's face stares out from the foliage on the south side, as if tormented by the pressure of the shafts.

In the north aisle are two ancient brasses, one of the Virgin, the other of Sir John Cassey and his wife, with her dog Terri at her feet. In the south aisle west window is 15th-century glass, including the much-reproduced depiction of St Catherine with her wheel under a flamboyant canopy. The church has several treasures of Saxon sculpture. On the interior wall of the tower is a relief of a Madonna and Child, dated to the 8th century. It once had painted details. The font is also Saxon, covered in trumpet-spiral ornament and reputedly one of the oldest surviving in England.

Outside the east end of the church, seen from the farmyard, are the footings of the Saxon apse. Arrows point upwards to an angel in relief, high on the wall, a rare survival of 10th-century carving. On the day of my visit, a pigeon had died and the ground beneath the angel was strewn as if with her fallen feathers. This is a church of constant delight and surprise.

Northleach

ST PETER AND ST PAUL
Perpendicular porch, wool merchants' brasses

Northleach was for more than a hundred years the pre-eminent Cotswold wool town. Annals of the merchants of the Calais Staple are filled with references to this market. Its wool was the finest and claimed the highest prices in Calais and Flanders. Accounts of life in the 15th century describe merchants constantly in transit between Northleach, the wharves of Stepney and the market at Calais. The town developed its own middle-men, the Midwinters, Busshes and Elmes, with whom the London dealers traded. Money flowed through the town, much of it finding its way to adorn a church that ranks with those of Cirencester and Chipping Campden.

The town today is a shadow of its mighty past, but not so its church. A sleepy square slopes upwards towards a churchyard that is hidden from view behind the town lock-up. Suddenly we are confronted with a bull-neck of a tower. This was built *c.*1380–1400 for an earlier church and rises over a later battery of pinnacles, battlements and tracery. The tower is decorated only on its upper stage, as if designed to be seen from a distance. Huge diagonal buttresses offer support, including two inside the nave itself.

Next we approach the great porch. Northleach porch may not be as ostentatious as Cirencester or as exotic as St Mary Redcliffe, Bristol, but its ogee hoods, buttresses and pinnacles are a perfect late-Gothic composition. The porch vault is of two bays, a flourish of ribs. Supporting it is a complete set of medieval corbel heads, including a cat playing a fiddle, above blind arcading. Overhead is a priest's chamber, with a fireplace and chimney hidden within a buttress and pinnacle. If such porches could talk, they could surely tell the history of a different England from that in any written record.

Northleach's interior is not worthy of its exterior. It has been maltreated by both the last two centuries, particularly the 20th. The original proportions survive. The ratio of height to length and width must be unprecedented in England, reminiscent of a Continental hall church. This impression is exaggerated by the clerestory, the huge tower arch and octagonal piers with concave faces. This design is rare but occurs elsewhere in the county, at Chipping Campden and Rendcomb. The nave was completed in the first half of the 15th century, possibly by Henry Winchcombe, a mason who carved his name on a pier base in the south arcade.

The clerestory was added by the wool magnate John Fortey. He raised the nave nearly half as high again as he found it. The Lady Chapel came later still in 1489, at a time when many chantries were founded in thanks for the end of the Wars of the Roses and the marriage of Henry Tudor to Elizabeth of York. The timber roofs and carved bosses are original. To lean back and gaze up at them (or use the mirror supplied for the purpose) is to experience the full majesty of English Perpendicular.

Northleach's brasses comprise the best collection in the county, having survived the iconoclasts, the vandals and the brass robbers. These mass-produced images reflected the status and interests of their patrons. Those at Northleach show not knights but merchants in con- temporary dress, and appear to make some attempt at truth to life. Some are bald, some bearded, some with lined faces, some still young. The figures are shown in prayer and most stand on the emblems of their wealth, the sheep and the woolpack.

Fortey himself (d.1459) is near the pulpit, splendid in a fur-lined gown and adorned with his woolmark. My favourite is the brass of John Taylour and his wife in the south aisle. They gaze towards each other, their fifteen children arrayed at their feet. His shoes are no longer pointed nor his hair long, indicating a later date for his death. Scholars have traced all these families and their interrelations. They constitute, as the guide says, 'members of an international trading organisation' as important to northern Europe as were the banking families of contemporary Florence or of Victorian London.

Northleach's modern furnishings are a mess. The new altar and the low-backed seating designed by Basil Spence in 1961 are out of character and insipid. A fussy iron screen divides the nave from the chancel. Perhaps a future age will find them less offensive to the eye.

St Mary Redcliffe, Bristol

REDCLIFFE WAY
Twin porches, Perpendicular interior, 1,200 roof bosses

'The fairest, goodliest and most famous parish church in England,' Queen Elizabeth is reputed to have said on a visit in 1574. Few would disagree, though some have questioned whether she said it. For centuries, St Mary's on its 'red cliff' welcomed home Bristol adventurers as they sailed up the Avon. Some are believed to have reached America before Columbus, based on a reference in Columbus's diaries.

St Mary's was the start and end of every such journey and no expense was spared on its adornment. Here the West Country tycoons, the Cabots, the Jays, the Canynges, the Ameryks, the Medes, sought glory in this world and security in the next. They built chantries to guard their souls in purgatory. They raised altars to their favourite saints. They financed clergy to sing Masses, twenty at the height of St Mary's prosperity. In 1416 a merchant named Belinus gave precious books in Latin to be read by the vicar and chaplains at their leisure. Fabrics, paintings, statues, icons and relics would have been carried up to the great porch from the forest of masts moored along the quay.

St Mary's is a masterpiece of English Gothic. It began as a shrine to Our Lady, on rising land by the river outside the city walls. Even today its spire of 292 ft (second only to Louth in Lincolnshire), restored in the 19th century after collapsing in the 15th, can hold its own among Bristol's tower blocks. But the tower must take second place to the north porch, a double-chambered structure facing what would have been the harbour. The inner porch, contemporary with St Mary's earliest phase, is Early Gothic while the outer porch, presumably built because the inner was overcrowded, is Decorated of the mid-14th century.

The outer porch is thus reached first. It is polygonal in plan and has an astonishing seven-pointed entrance arch. Scholars regard this as oriental, its origins lying in documents brought back by travellers from the Near East and Moorish Spain. Jean Bony, historian of English Decorated, describes the stonework as 'undercut in the manner of oriental ivories and criss-crossed by a pattern of large diamonds, suggesting ivory box lids'. Michael Quinton Smith, in his history of the church, sees in the porch's deep-carved motifs all the 'luxuriance of Seljuk portals in Asia Minor or the stucco-work of Islamic Spain'. By the early 14th century, English taste was no longer slave to France. It was open to the trade winds.

Who designed this marvel? We know that its motifs recur in medieval psalters. We know that one 'Robert the Sculptor' was in the retinue of an expedition sent to Persia by Edward I, which visited the Masjid Camii at Isfahan. That Persian temple vault is strikingly similar to the Lady Chapel at Wells. Others detect the hand of the master mason of late Decorated, William Ramsay. There is a similar 'oriental' door, possibly by Ramsay, at Cley next the Sea (Norfolk). He died in the Black Death in 1349, and this exotic cosmopolitanism vanished into English Perpendicular.

The richness of this porch can be seen in every detail. The polygonal buttresses are embellished with nodding ogee arches. The outside niches carry contorted images of pilgrims, cripples and peasants, a photographic record of those who would have loitered on this spot six centuries ago. The window tracery is like angels' wings. Inside, the hexagonal vault is so ribbed as to appear spinning free of the corners. Nor is the inner porch any less impressive. The view into it from the outer porch is as down a tunnel into history. The black Purbeck shafts and the 'windblown' stiff-leaf capitals are superb, the alcoves only awaiting the return of distant sailors and their offerings.

The first impression of the interior is of sheer Perpendicularity. Every line searches upwards to the roof where it fractures into a maze of vault ribs. Yet the structure is a combination of inconsistencies, joins, changes in style and level. These add to St Mary's appeal, each age making its distinctive mark. The plan is that of an Early Gothic church, but a massive rebuilding on the old foundations began in the early years of the 14th century, yielding a Decorated south aisle and transept. The rest of the church dates from the end of that century and is Perpendicular. Yet these periods seem immaterial. The whole interior is a forest of soaring arches and vaults with aisles swerving away on all sides, including in the transepts.

The church is vaulted throughout. Palm-like pier shafts push upwards to the vault interrupted by only a hint of a capital. The vault ribs form astonishing patterns, lozenges in the nave, hexagons in the south aisle, squares in the transepts and rectangles in the choir. The patterns are punctuated, so we are told, by no fewer than 1,200 bosses. It is as if the master masons had sat with their sketchbooks and doodled a dozen cat's cradles, then tossed the plan to their carvers and told them to 'go and decorate it'. In the north nave aisle is a boss in the form of a circular maze.

Facing the entrance on the south wall of the nave aisle are three tomb recesses, their canopies similar to the 'oriental' north doorway. These recesses are Gothic at its most exhilarating, swaying and bouncing concave lines swooping out to huge foliated stops. They were intended to house the tombs of priests of the 14th-century foundation. One contains that of John Lavyngton (d.1411). Similar tomb recesses are in Bristol Cathedral, where they are painted.

The church's principal benefactor, William Canynges, lived from 1402 to 1474 and thus saw both the completion of the interior and its restoration following the collapse of the old tower in 1446. Canynges was a merchant in cloth, shipping and property. He was Mayor of Bristol five times and its Member of Parliament. His list of ships is recorded in the church, and he employed 800 men in Bristol alone. On the death of his wife in 1467 he decided to become a priest and was ordained. As a result, he is portrayed twice: once alongside his wife in their tomb in the south transept, in the rich garments of a 15th-century merchant, and again nearby as a priest. At the feet of Canynges as merchant lies a dog; at the feet of Canynges as priest is an infidel's head.

The stained glass at St Mary's is Victorian, apart from some medieval fragments near the tower and a rather insipid modern window in the Lady Chapel by H. J. Stammers. My preference is for the Comper work in the south transept, but the glass throughout detracts from the architecture. An iron screen of 1710, once dividing nave and chancel and now beneath the tower, is the masterpiece of William Edney. To Sacheverell Sitwell it was 'one of the splendours of the ignored baroque art of England'. The finial is of two elongated arms holding a snake and a balance.

St Mary's in the 18th century also produced the tragedy of Thomas Chatterton. Above the porch is the room where the boy poet is alleged to have delved among church records to write his 'forged' document on medieval Bristol. He moved to London on the strength of its initial success, committing suicide at the age of seventeen. Chatterton's father was sexton to St Mary's.

Tewkesbury

OLD BAPTIST CHAPEL
Chapel in converted medieval house

The chapel is open to the public and still available for worship. It lies in a small courtyard off Church Street, directly opposite the abbey. A medieval timber-framed house was converted for chapel use probably in the

1620s. It retains beams that date from the 15th century. This is one of the earliest Baptist chapels in England.

That said, the main facade is mostly 18th century. The interior was altered in the 1720s to provide a minister's room on the upper floor. It was then that the elegant windows were installed, bringing light to the interior. The Baptistery is a (concealed) pit directly in front of the pulpit. The guide points out that the gradual adaptation of a family dwelling to a place of worship illustrates 'the belief that religion should be centred around the family and home as opposed to the monumental churches and rather impersonal clergy'. The raised pulpit, the gallery and minister's room evoke a tradition of group worship in which the congregation takes full part in the ceremony. The warm sunlight pouring in through high Georgian windows makes it a tranquil respite from the bustling town outside.

Hampshire

Romsey

ABBEY OF ST MARY AND ST ETHELFLAEDA
Saxon roods, Norman arcades, carved capitals

The abbey was founded by King Alfred's son Edward as a nunnery in 907. It was sacked by Danes, rebuilt by Saxons and again by Normans, each time as a centre for female worship and education. At the Dissolution the abbey was acquired by the town. This saved it from demolition and, because of its size, from any need for subsequent expansion. Its setting is marred by mediocre town houses and shops pressing on three sides. The exterior, mostly crumbling or restored Norman work, is patchy and the interior strangely empty. The abbey lacks the bustle of a cathedral yet is too big for the bustle of a small parish. Yet Romsey is one of England's grandest Norman churches.

On the outside wall of the south transept is the Romsey rood, a pre-Conquest relief of Christ, His arms spread in welcome not in crucifixion. The hand of God appears from a cloud above His head. Next to it is the magnificent doorway that once led to the abbess's cloisters, adorned with rosettes and twisted shafts. Apart from the later east and west windows, the interior retains its Norman appearance. Chancel, crossing, transepts and nave are tall and white, and massively proportioned. Arches pile on one another in three decks of arcade, gallery and clerestory. The piers have multiple shafts, one of which runs the entire height of the bay. The gallery has odd sub-arches with wall passages.

There is an intriguing evolution of style as we progress westwards from the crossing down the nave. The first two bays are divided by a cylindrical pier of two tiers. This form did not last long, since the next bays appear to have reverted to the standard Norman design. The westernmost bays, however, are Early Gothic, their piers resting on smart Purbeck bases and rising to capitals of stiff-leaf interspersed with faces. Gothic also are the two final bays of the gallery and almost the entire nave clerestory.

A closer look at the details reveals Romsey's phenomenal variety. Capitals are decorated with heads, beasts or flowers. Corbels erupt with faces peering down on the congregation. Two capitals in the chancel aisles tell stories, one of two kings pulling each other's beard, the other of kings and angels, with an inscription stating that its carver was called Robert. Everywhere are signs of 12th-century masons eagerly trying new styles and motifs imported from France.

Romsey offers a rich gallery of art of all periods. In the chancel south aisle chapel is a screen containing another Saxon rood, a finely executed Crucifixion with angels and saints in strong relief. Two soldiers are at the foot of the cross, one offering the sponge with vinegar. Romsey can justly claim this as one of the finest Saxon works extant in England. In the retro-choir is the coffin lid of a medieval abbess, her hand eerily emerging from beneath it to hold fast to her wand of office.

The north aisle and transept were, until the Dissolution, used as a parish church by the townspeople and an outer aisle was added, the transept acting as a chancel. Screens divided this area off from the rest of the abbey to stop the nuns 'escaping'. By the time of the Dissolution they numbered only nineteen, while the parish aisle must have been packed. When the old abbey was bought by the town (for £100) the additional aisle was demolished and Perpendicular windows inserted in the old north wall. Such was the parlous state of these buildings in the 18th century that the north transept was used as a fire station and the north aisle was a school. I sometimes wonder if many under-used modern churches might not benefit from being placed at the service of their wider community today.

Today the north transept retains a rare painted reredos of the early 16th century. Near the north door is a memorial effigy to a little child of the town named Alice Taylor, who succumbed to scarlet fever in 1843. She died clutching a rose her father gave her from his garden, and is portrayed on her deathbed, the rose still in her hand. In the south transept is the simple floor plate to Lord Mountbatten whose house was nearby at Broadlands.

Herefordshire

Abbey Dore

Transitional capital carvings,
17th-century screen and gallery

The first impression of Abbey Dore down the Golden
Valley is of a corner of France delicately dropped into
an English meadow. The dark Hereford sandstone is
speckled with white lime. The nave has gone, but the
transepts, crossing and chancel of the old Cistercian
abbey church loom high and austere. The French order
was dedicated to asceticism, locating its monasteries far
from settlement or temptation. Today, Abbey Dore is in
a most sublime spot.

The monastery was founded in 1147, but most of what
we see today is a rebuilding begun in 1180. The church
is thus Herefordshire's exemplar of the transition from
Norman to Early Gothic. While the exterior is red, the
interior is of cool, grey limestone, brought to flaming
life when a late sun shines low across the transept.
Although the exterior is bare, the interior, with its 17th-
century fittings, is sumptuous. The dominant feature is
the east end, which shows Early Gothic at its most
developed. A low arcade behind the altar has clusters of
shafts, fourteen to each bay, with a double ambulatory
and lancet windows behind. These all soar upwards in

an astonishing rush, to meet the main east window, a lofty triple lancet with similar lavish shafts and mouldings. If this is ascetic, then I am Cistercian.

The chancel has a wonderful stone-flagged floor, on which rise arcades adorned with a wealth of late Norman and Early Gothic capitals and bosses. These can be seen both *in situ* and among the ruined fragments gathered in the ambulatory. They capture the 'Transitional moment', when the carvers' motifs were Norman but the architectural setting already had rib vaults and pointed arches. Norman scallops flower into trumpet shapes, into water-leaf and finally into the stiff-leaf of Early Gothic. The ambulatory is a forest of ancient carving, with the walls dividing the outer aisles into chapels left unfinished. On a dark evening we can imagine the masons sitting here with the latest pattern-books from France, talking over the designs, chipping with their chisels and pushing forward the frontiers of their art.

After the Dissolution, Abbey Dore fell into ruin. Not until the 1630s did it revive, when the local Scudamore family rescued it for the parish under the High Church influence of Archbishop Laud. A battlemented tower was raised, a touch of England on the French exterior. Stained glass was inserted in the east lancet windows. The Scudamores happily chose a talented carpenter, John Abel (1577–1664), whose Herefordshire work included Leominster town hall. He crafted the mighty wooden chancel roof and raised a screen, *c.*1633, to enclose the congregational area. This screen is a splendid example of 17th-century classicism, heavy and rich, a squirearchy

Baroque in celebration of the manor, the church and the (Stuart) crown.

Against the west wall is a wonderfully solid oak gallery, warming what might otherwise be a gaunt space.

Kilpeck

ST MARY AND ST DAVID
Norman carving

Kilpeck is widely regarded as England's most perfect Norman church. It sits unobtrusively on a mound next to a castle ruin between the Wye and Dore valleys. The view is west to the Black Mountains and east to the Malverns. Lit by a setting sun, Kilpeck's red walls seem to take fire and fill the Marches with rich glowing embers.

The church was adjacent to a Benedictine priory and remains as built, a Norman structure of nave, chancel and apse, with no aisles or tower. Nothing appears to have been added or subtracted over the centuries, apart from the furnishings. This means that the carvings are *in situ* and in context. They cover the south and west doorways, the chancel arch and the corbel-table that runs round the entire church. Dating from the mid 12th century, they are masterpieces of the Herefordshire School, ranking with the fonts at Eardisley and Castle Frome. For their survival we must thank the durability of Old Red Sandstone, salvation of Herefordshire architecture, which seems impervious to weather.

The Kilpeck carvings demonstrate the vigour of the Saxon–Norman sculptural tradition. Themes and styles are drawn from the pilgrim routes across northern

Europe, from Vikings, Saxons, Celts, Franks and Spaniards, the entire 'Northmen' diaspora. The south doorway has a Tree of Life tympanum. Oriental warriors peer through the foliage in the shafts and the dragons in the jambs. No less intriguing, if less accomplished, are the grotesques of the corbel-table, best preserved round the apse. Some are abstract, some figurative, some mythical. Here is an explicit sheela-na-gig of a woman holding open her vagina, a pig upside down, a dog and rabbit, two doves, musicians, wrestlers and acrobats. All the life of a busy and bawdy Herefordshire village is depicted on its church, with no respect for the decorum piety.

The interior is whitewashed in the post-Reformation style, and is Norman in style but not atmosphere. The carvings remain superb. In the shafts of the chancel arch are elongated saints, three to each side. These are quite different from the figures on the outside, stylised, serene, almost Gothic. This superimposing of sculpted figures on the shafts is found at Ferrara in Italy but not in England. Next door is a water stoup, apparently depicting a pregnant woman holding her belly. The font is so big it could be used as a bath.

At the west end of the church is a Jacobean gallery, perhaps the most English artefact in the place.

Ledbury

ST MICHAEL
'Floating' Norman chancel,
Decorated baptistery chapel

Ledbury is an attractive town, set tight against a limb of the Malverns. From a distance its church spire appears to be pinning Ledbury to the slope. Once we are in the town, the church is suddenly unobtrusive, shut off from the hubbub of the high street and reached through a rabbit-warren of tiny lanes.

The steeple is a work of architecture in its own right, detached from the church to the north. It dates from the early 13th century, its spire replaced in the 18th by a Worcester architect named Nathaniel Wilkinson. Ledbury is thus a church of all periods. The west front is basically Norman, with turrets and zigzag carvings round its doorway. Inside, the eye is immediately drawn to the piers of the 12th-century chancel arcades, which stand like tree trunks, holding up rough-hewn limestone walls with porthole clerestory windows. This chancel was left stranded by succeeding generations of builders, and looks like a church within a church. It is in the most blood-thirsty Norman, framed by a subsided chancel arch that seems about to give up the ghost.

Round this chancel, the Gothic masons conduct their courtly dance. The aisles are large and airy, the same width as the nave but appearing bigger and grander by continuing on both sides of the chancel and thus embracing it with majestic windows. The whole interior is dominated by these windows, marvels of the Decorated era. They are mostly in the familiar Herefordshire style of 'three-light Reticulated' or 'stepped-lancet'. Most are filled with Victorian and later stained glass.

Even finer windows light the north chancel chapel. It was designed as a chapter house in 1330, at a time when the Benedictines hoped to convert Ledbury into a collegiate church. The chapel was later used as a baptistery. The windows are splendid accumulations of quatrefoils piled on trefoils, with ballflower enlivening every shaft. The exterior is as ornate as the interior. Only Leominster can compete with this richness.

Every corner of the church has a distinctive character. The nave is floored with inscribed memorial slabs. An effigy of a Benedictine monk at prayer stands under a canopy in the chapel. There are two fonts, one 17th-century Baroque, the other Gothic by George Gilbert Scott. In the sanctuary is a monument to the Skynners, with Mrs Skynner in an Elizabethan ruff but a hat that might pass muster at Ascot. There are also monuments by Westmacott, Flaxman and Thornycroft.

Ledbury has a remarkable sanctuary opening visible only from a specific point in the nave near the chancel. A red glass window is set above the east window, thought to have been a substitute for the red sanctuary lamp banned at the Reformation. In the north aisle is the modern Heaton window by John Clark. It rises up the wall like a furious flame, paying no respect to its surroundings. The churchwarden denied it was controversial, but conceded that it was 'much discussed'. Next to it is one of the many Georgian copies of the Sir

Joshua Reynolds windows at New College, Oxford, with Lady Reynolds as Faith and the actress Mrs Siddons as Hope.

Leominster

ST PETER AND ST PAUL
Norman tower, Decorated south aisle windows, ducking stool

The old priory lay away from the centre of the town. What is left of the priory church is tucked down a quiet cul-de-sac in what amounts to its own park. It is a fragment, but a superb one. The west end, consisting of Norman north nave and aisle, and adjacent parochial south nave and aisle, survived the Reformation. The present church thus comprises three large chambers plus a north aisle, each dating from a distinct era of English architecture. The view from the south-west displays every period in a magnificent array of building styles.

The prominent Norman tower does not soar, but is a magnificent part of Leominster's splendid western aspect. It stands to the left, its base is complete with arched windows and carved doorway, apparently of the Herefordshire School. The 'school' trademark includes monsters and a strange man with quilted trousers. To its left are the Early Gothic lancets of the north aisle; to its right is the Perpendicular window of the south nave; farther right again is the Decorated west window of the south aisle, its arches studded with ballflower. These last decorative flourishes enjoyed a brief burst of fashion as Decorated reached its apogee around 1300.

The south elevation of the church is a coherent Decorated design. Five majestic windows, again framed in ballflower, are filled with Geometrical tracery, but with the circular lights cusped into a series of stars. The effect has the delicacy of lace yet the strength of stone. These are windows of the first rank.

The interior of Leominster is as exciting as the exterior. To the north lies the old Norman nave, built for the parishioners while the monks occupied the now-vanished chancel. This part of the church is flanked by elephantine arcades topped by expanses of raw masonry. Height is achieved by simply piling tier upon tier. The 13th century brought the new south nave for the parish, and the 14th saw the addition of the present south aisle. The dividing arcade was rebuilt in the 17th century and again in the 19th. It contains a superb 14th-century piscina and sedilia group, again enriched with ballflower but with triangular hoods rather than the ogees of the late Decorated style.

Most of the early furnishings were lost in a great fire which virtually gutted the church in 1699. However, Leominster possesses the last ducking stool to be used in England, kept in the north aisle. In 1809 Jenny Pipes was ducked in the local river, whether as a 'scold' or as a saleswoman caught for selling adulterated goods, is not recorded.

Huntingdon

Barnack

ST JOHN
Saxon tower, stiff-leaf font, Christ in Majesty carving

Most Saxon churches are celebrated more for being old than for being beautiful. They are for the archaeologist rather than the layman. Not so Barnack. Its Saxon tower and Early Gothic spire form the most pleasing composition in the county. Barnack was famous for its stone, the pale pinkish limestone of the western Fens, beloved of medieval carvers in these parts as was Ham stone in Somerset.

The tower has vertical and horizontal strips, with triangular windows in its west front. The corners have familiar Saxon long-and-short stones and the door surrounds come with discordant capitals above their pillars. Above rises the disciplined symmetry of the Early Gothic steeple, composed of pinnacles rising out of broaches round an octagonal belfry. This is crowned with a short but virile stone cap. 'If it is called a spire,' writes Pevsner, 'it must be one of the earliest in England.' It dates from c.1200 and is a structure of real power.

We enter through a superb Early Gothic porch, with a steeply pitched roof and fine stiff-leaf capitals to the doorway. Inside, the tower arch resumes the Saxon theme. It rests on abaci between the piers and the arch which look as if the mason thought of them only at the last minute. The style of these abaci is reminiscent of the Art Deco of a 1930s liner, or even a stack of hamburgers. I have never seen such capitals anywhere else – although there are echoes in the arch at neighbouring Wittering.

The remainder of the interior seems not quite under control. The nave is Transitional. The north arcade has late-Norman stiff-leaf capitals and a few human heads. The south arcade moves easily into Early Gothic, with more stiff-leaf, clustered shafts, chamfered arches but nothing so vulgar as human heads. The restoration by Leslie T. Moore is dominated by the Victorian pews and rood screen, the latter using 15th-century panels for a dado. In the chancel is a wall memorial to Francis Whitstone, who died in 1598. Four of his seven sons ranged behind him are carved, the others meriting only paint.

Not an inch of wallspace in this church seems to lack some point of interest. The chancel piscina has a nodding ogee arch, projecting so far that it must have banged the head of the priest. Monsters peer out from the sedilia. The Lady Chapel has big niches either side of the altar, both early 16th century. The statue of the Virgin and Child is modern, but the Annunciation is original and of the finest quality. The font is outstanding, and rare in displaying stiff-leaf foliage. Patterns cover the bowl surface with almost rococo delicacy. It is set on a stem with a graceful, trefoil-headed arcade. The bowl itself is deep and may have been intended for the total immersion of the infant.

At the east end of the north aisle is Barnack's masterpiece, a seated Christ in Majesty discovered under the floor in 1931. Now generally dated before the Conquest, its strong face and flowing garments are among the most striking sculptures of the period in England.

Castor

ST KYNEBURGHA
Exterior Norman carvings, angel roof,
St Catherine wall painting

Castor sits in a discreet suburb of Peterborough, on the slope of a hill above the bank of the River Nene. It was an outpost of neighbouring Peterborough Cathedral and is a minor masterpiece of Norman architecture, dominated by a magnificent crossing tower that merits the title of sister to that of Peterborough. The tower is ornamented with two tiers of arcading, some blind and some with paired openings, all carved with zigzags, billets, fish scale, lozenges: in other words the full Norman works.

The rest of the exterior is equally rich in Norman carving. In the south chancel wall is a priest's doorway, with a niche and simple tympanum giving the date of dedication as 1124 (though the 24 appears to have been scratched in later). It is flanked by a Perpendicular window, an Early Gothic lancet and windows with Geometrical and Y-tracery. Castor is thus a textbook of medieval architecture. Above the south porch is a Norman Christ in benediction. Inside is a gnarled oak door, the sort that is a pleasure to find unlocked and push open.

The interior is worthy of the exterior. The nave arcades are Transitional, with piers beneath just-pointed arches. The low crossing is pure Norman, with clustered piers and capitals depicting beasts and vegetation. These are more than mere faces. One depicts a man gathering fruit while another shows the legend of St Kyneburgha: when she was being chased by two thugs intent on rape, the contents of her basket spilled out and sprang instantly into bushes. These most conveniently trapped the men in their branches.

The roof is alive with freshly painted angels carrying musical instruments and the keys of St Peter. They look like primitive fairground ornaments but are said to be accurate to their 15th-century originals. The south transept has tall windows and clear glass, revealing the sky over the Nene. This transept contained the village school until the 1890s. The north transept held the shrine of St Kyneburgha and is divided from the north aisle by a heavy-traceried stone screen of the 1330s.

Castor's chancel contains many treasures, including a Norman piscina, an Early Gothic piscina and sedilia, and a delicate Saxon carving of an apostle. At the back of the north aisle is an admirably clear wall painting of St Catherine on her wheel, with the philosophers whom she is said to have converted being executed. It is the only picture I know of philosophers being put to death.

Castor sets its embroidered kneelers on the pew shelves. This fills the nave with colour, as the angels do the roof.

Kent

Barfreston

ST NICHOLAS
Complete Norman decoration

The village sits snugly in a defile a mile from the North
Downs Way. I visited it on a winter day when the hill
outside the church was so clogged with snow as to have
become impassable. The adjacent pub with log fire and
hot soup was as welcome as the sight of Barfreston's
celebrated carvings. The church is situated on a small
bluff with its west end giving directly onto the pub
garden. It is a simple, double-cell chapel covered with
Norman decoration, earning it the title of the 'Kilpeck of
the South'. Heavy but apparently necessary 19th-century
restoration has deprived Barfreston's interior of some of
its aura of antiquity.

The south doorway can scarcely be rivalled in England
for rich and well-preserved late Norman carving. In the
tympanum, Christ is flanked by a king and queen, angels
and graceful figures in foliage. The first and second
surrounding orders have more carved foliage, and roundels with animal musicians and other chimeras. The
outer order has ovals with the signs of the zodiac and
the Labours of the Months. These are important to
scholars of Norman iconography, and also appear round

Thomas à Becket's shrine at Canterbury. Becket may even be the bishop at the apex of the middle order. Churches this near to Canterbury would have been in the thick of his cult.

The outside walls have an almost continuous arcading, some blind, some fenestrated. Above is a complete corbel-table of carved heads. The east end has three round-headed windows buried in lesser arches and above a wheel window of eight spokes composed of tiny columns. On either side are fragments of evangelists and even a knight on horseback. To one side is a lion. This wall is one of Kent's cheeriest compositions.

The tall interior is a casket of Norman art. The chancel arch has twisted columns, rippling foliage and 'swallow-tail spur' bases, of the sort which occur in the choir at Canterbury. On either side are high niches for now-vanished altars. The nave has two carved string courses, at sill and window arch height. These appear to have abstract decoration, but on closer inspection reveal wilful variety. A frieze of animals breaks into the pattern on the north wall, while more animals form stops to the south windows. The chancel courses are even richer. The wheel window surround is decorated with a wealth of abstract and animal ornament.

Barfreston is dated to the last quarter of the 12th century, the last flourish of Norman art before the advent of Gothic. We can already see in the capitals of the chancel arch traces of the transition from water-leaf to stiff-leaf. But mostly this church looks back not forward, to the France of the Norman Conquest rather than the Gothic one.

Lincolnshire

Boston

ST BOTOLPH
The Stump, lantern interior, 62 misericords

Boston's famous Stump is not only Lincolnshire's most celebrated landmark and lighthouse to the Fens. It is also a wonder of medieval engineering. At 272 ft it is the highest church tower, not counting spires, in England. When the tower was planned in the 1300s, the town was the premier wool port in England after London. Status required a church and a beacon to match. Though massive in its foundations, the tower remained vulnerable to Fenland clay and was not felt to be strong enough to support a spire: hence the octagon and the nickname.

The Stump is traditionally photographed from along the banks of the River Witham, the structure rising vertically from the sloping foreshore. This view has been spoiled by concrete piling of the banks and by the building of a modern bridge and police station directly opposite. Today the view from the market to the east is happier, with the added advantage that from here the tower rises above a forest of pinnacles and does not overpower the nave.

Work on a new church was begun in 1309, with the Decorated style in full flower, but the tower was not finished until two centuries later. The tower's diminutive west doorway is Decorated, but Perpendicularity, in every sense, soon asserts itself. Blind panelling soars upwards past three windows on the north, west and south faces. Then come two ogee windows for the original bell-chamber. From here a spire should have taken over, as at Louth. At this point, says Pevsner, 'hubris gripped the Bostonians and they decided to heighten their tower . . . an undeniable coarsening'. The higher bell-stage is a rough-and-ready work of architecture. Although there is no specific evidence of a planned spire, having not built one, the masons seemed to have gone on building up for the sake of sheer height. But once the disappointing bell-stage is passed, the crowning octagon is a superb work, adorned with pinnacles and flying buttresses. This was not completed until well into the 16th century.

If the remainder of the exterior is spectacular, the interior is overwhelming. The original south doors to the nave are among the finest medieval doors to survive anywhere. Boston is 14th-century design at its most generous, mobile and symmetrical. The view east from the west end of the nave is of grand arcades and colourful roofs. The eye is led through a graceful Decorated chancel arch into what is almost an optical illusion, the sham vault of the chancel. This was rebuilt in the 18th century and a new east window inserted in the 19th. Its tracery is Lincolnshire Decorated, its lines swirling upwards with manic freedom, in contrast to the static Panel tracery of Perpendicular, copied apparently from the tracery on the south doors.

The view west is no less exhilarating. The tower interior is as grand as the exterior, a vaulted lantern open to the top of the second stage and encompassing a breathtaking space. The view upwards in the early evening light is like peering into the canopy of a rain forest. The famous climb to the top of the lantern has the same number of steps as there are days of the year. The entrance is guarded by an 18th-century iron screen.

The medieval and Victorian furnishings of Boston are rich. In the north aisle is a black marble slab commemorating a merchant from Munster, who died at the height of the town's prosperity in 1312. A window in the east chapel includes scenes from Boston history, including the departure of its citizens in 1630 to found Boston in Massachusetts. They were seen off by the town's Nonconformist vicar, John Cotton, who was to follow them in 1633. His magnificent pulpit still stands in the nave, minutely carved with Ionic columns, picked out with finials and gilding. From here he would preach two-hour sermons and conduct five-hour catechisms.

A year after Cotton's departure to America, Archbishop Laud arrived to reassert the old rite, founding a splendid library above the porch. The chapel at the west end of the south aisle was named after Cotton in 1857. When George Gilbert Scott wanted to paint its ceiling with stars and stripes the vicar felt this was going too far.

Finest of the furnishings are in the chancel. Here George Pace in the 20th century added canopies to the 14th-century stalls. There is a superb collection of 62 original misericords, one of a monk birching a boy. In the aisle roof is a roof boss of a white elephant, recalling the bring-and-buy sale by which money was raised for its restoration. Boston has one of the most extravagant fonts in Decorated Gothic style in the country. It is by E. W. Pugin and could be a centrepiece for a fruiterer's wedding.

Brant Broughton

ST HELEN
Porch carving and gargoyles, interior by Bodley

Brant Broughton is remarkable for two contrasting reasons. The exterior is enlivened with superb 14th-century decoration, a gallery of Gothic carving to rank with Heckington and Sleaford. The interior is of the same period, but deferentially restored by a Victorian rector in collusion with the architect, G. F. Bodley. Together they represent a model of original Gothic and Gothic revival in harmonious alliance, both carried out by local craftsmen. Brant Broughton is an example of what might have been done with so many 19th-century ruins that were butchered or destroyed.

The steeple is magnificent, a fine tower rising to a soaring, exhilarating spire. It is set back minimally behind the parapet. The crocketed outline and attendant pinnacles, slightly askew, shoot the eye upwards when seen from directly below. Even the lucarnes are kept small to avoid interrupting the ascent. These structures have as much art and artifice as a Greek column. The Decorated tower, built just before the Black Death, is balanced by a symmetrical composition of nave and aisles added in the Perpendicular style. Even the porches match, north and south. Everywhere is ballflower and fleurons, scattered like petals across the face of the church.

These porches are gems of 14th-century architecture. They are stone vaulted with bosses and encrusted with animated carving. The bosses are so big as almost to fill the vault. Green Men guard the doors. These carvings are more than a menagerie, rather an imaginative realm in which mischief, humour and repulsion seem as important as piety. So lifelike are many of the faces, so simple their tasks, like a sower or a drummer boy, that they must surely be portraits. Yet they lie alongside monstrous beasts and distorted flowers. Over the south porch a man has his shirt raised and bottom exposed, apparently defecating at the viewer. What on earth was in the carver's mind? All of human life is in these carvings from the most vital period of English vernacular art.

The second Brant Broughton is inside, the careful application of Victorian restoration to medieval architecture. As at Algarkirk, the stimulus was a new Victorian squarson, the Anglo-Catholic Canon Frederick Sutton, who arrived in 1873. His architect was Bodley and his later partner, Thomas Garner. Together they played a brilliant variation on a Decorated theme. The only sadness is that a 20th-century restoration did not correct one Victorian blindspot, the scraping of the walls. These remain partly scraped and unnecessarily stained and gloomy. They need limewash.

Sutton and Bodley's innovations in the nave mostly took the form of iron candelabras and the insertion of window glass. The ironwork was made at the local Coldron forge in the village, which is still in business.

Sutton's glass is most accomplished. He took advice from Kempe but designed the works himself and prepared the glass in a kiln set up in the adjacent rectory. The only exception is the east window by Burlison & Grylls and some of the south windows are later. But the uniformity of design and the simplicity of the colours are gloriously at peace with the architecture.

The chancel is more obviously Bodley's work and replaced a Georgian structure standing at the time of Sutton's arrival. He was then working on his masterpiece at Hoar Cross (Staffs) in a spirit of Tractarian grandeur. Behind the screen rises a typically Bodleyesque lierne-ribbed vault, wooden and brilliantly painted. By him too are the choir stalls, organ case, pulpit and reredos, the last framing a 15th-century German painted panel given by Sutton. It is a serenely sophisticated space to find in such robust surroundings. Under the tower is a superb fragment of a 14th-century Trinity sculpture.

Grantham

ST WULFRAM
Steeple and west front, Decorated tracery,
corbel-table carvings

Here is the finest steeple in England. When seen from the railway or across the flatlands of west Lincolnshire, Grantham's slender spike is one of the most exhilarating images of English Gothic. Nothing subsequently erected, even in glorious Somerset, is quite its equal among churches. Only the spire of Salisbury Cathedral can stand comparison. Yet Grantham has always been a parish church, its majesty civic, not ecclesiastical. The 19th century was hard on the interior and 20th-century glass adds aggression to the offence. The church is more awesome than lovable. But the steeple is to be savoured, best approached from the west past a prettified close of gardens and trees.

The quality of English church towers lies in the mason's ability to resolve horizontal and vertical elements. The best towers in the east Midlands were earlier than those of East Anglia and Somerset, yet seem to have achieved this resolution in advance. At Grantham, the tower begins as a classic work of the turn of the 14th century. The multiple mouldings of the west doorway are echoed in the main west window, which has Intersecting tracery. Both are embellished in ballflower decoration of *c.*1300. The flanking end windows of the north and south aisles are filled with the most elaborate Geometrical tracery.

The tower now rises free of the roofline of the aisles, with two tiers of blind arcading. Then come two stages of bell-openings, one with two windows, the next with just one, as if to increase the tension. The tower is carefully tapered, with lines accentuated by angle buttresses. Four pinnacles now effortlessly conceal the shift from square tower into octagonal spire, which rises from its small broaches in a single final thrust. The taper of the spire seems perfectly judged, with its ribs and three tiers of diminishing lucarnes covered in ballflower, as if infested with golden snails. Grantham's tower ranks with any masterpiece of English art. Such was the effect on Ruskin that he (allegedly) swooned on first seeing it.

The interior of Grantham is a single vast rectangle,

its atmosphere dominated by George Gilbert Scott's Victorian roofs and rood screen and by the gloomy stained glass that fills most of the windows. The arcades are a dignified jigsaw puzzle, the central four bays surviving in part from an earlier Norman church that was ruined in a mighty fire when hit by lightning in 1222. These include Norman piers and capitals, with water-leaf and scalloped carvings.

Greatest of the post-fire innovations, apart from the steeple, were the aisle windows. These present a sequence of English tracery through its finest era, roughly from 1280 to the advent of Perpendicular *c.*1350. The earliest are six Geometrical windows of *c.*1280 in the north aisle. Contemporary with these is the north doorway (inside the later north porch, now the bookshop): this is a sumptuous portal of shafting and stiff-leaf. The tracery in the south nave aisle is Intersecting, first cusped and then, as we move eastwards, curvilinear with ballflower. The south chancel aisle windows are of 1330–50, each a variant on the most flowing Gothic style. The eye can hardly follow the line desired by the mason: we would love to have seen these patterns being planned and replanned in the workshop sand.

After this excitement the rest of Grantham may seem an anticlimax. Much of the Victorian glass is of high quality. The Kempe work is recognisable. Wailes contributed the west windows and Blomfield the reredos, a work that matches the grandeur of its setting. Above the south porch is a chained library, open in summer.

Less noticeable is the remarkable corbel-table also retained from the pre-fire church. It surrounds most of the exterior wall, especially on the south side, offering an extraordinary gallery of medieval carving. These grotesques are everywhere, extending beyond the customary gargoyles and corbels to include figures inserted apparently at random. Some are tiny, some monstrous, some human, some embracing each other. Some have fingers in their mouths, some are smiling, others sneering. Gazing up at them – Ruskin's 'monstrous and loathsome heads in clownish stupidity' – we can only wonder at what inspired their creators to take such trouble over what appear such trifles.

Heckington

ST ANDREW
Decorated figure carvings, Easter Sepulchre

The exterior of Heckington ranks with Brant Broughton among Lincolnshire's galleries of vernacular art. It stands in the centre of its village, a testament to the imagination of the early 14th century, to the years of ingenuity and plenty before the Black Death. The principal benefactor was its rector, Richard de Potesgrave, chaplain to Edward III and thus a man of means. The true heroes of Heckington are the carvers themselves, men of humour, intelligence and artistic licence. We have no knowledge of who they were, but they speak to us from every gargoyle and corbel head. A frame in the chancel shows a collection of the masons' marks. Imagine a modern artist consenting to remain so anonymous.

Of the tower a harsh critic might say that it is too solid. Heavy buttresses hold it to the ground and the

broach pinnacles, each a delightfully ornamented octagon, are too heavy for the spire. That said, the structure
sustains a wealth of carvings, including 38 statues. The
south elevation of the church itself is alive with figures,
the porch likewise, inside and out. Monsters leap from
foliage. Angels jostle peasants. A series of figures seem
to be skiing downhill under the gargoyles. Many of the
faces appear true to life. This must be a satirical magazine
as well as an art gallery. The windows are equally superb
and best appreciated from outside. In each the upward
line seems to follow a different path. The climax is the
chancel east window. Its tracery is curvilinear, describing
tulips or pincers according to imaginative fancy.

The interior of Heckington is at first a disappointment.
The scraped walls are black, streaked and crying out
for plaster. Here is one Lincolnshire church which the
Victorians did not handle well. The nave is redeemed by
the Decorated font, as richly foliated as the porch but
sadly stripped of statues. Some relief is in the chancel. It
contains the tomb of Richard de Potesgrave, with the
county's finest grouping of Easter Sepulchre, sedilia and
piscina. The Sepulchre is a masterpiece. Unlike Hawton
(Notts), the composition is vertical, with the figures
recessed behind architectural features. The soldiers sleep-
ing outside the tomb are almost hidden inside their
canopies. The superstructure is a mass of foliage, as if
the masons wanted to hide the shrine in a forest.

The same hands were clearly at work on the sedilia
opposite. Here the imagery varies from pretty statues of
saints to scenes from village life. We see a mediator
trying to settle a domestic quarrel, a woman with a

squirrel and a boy feeding a bird. At the back of the church is an excellent exhibition of its history.

Louth

ST JAMES
Tallest steeple, nave corbel heads, medieval chests

Louth possesses the most perfect Perpendicular Gothic steeple in England, rivalling Suffolk's Stoke-by-Nayland and the aristocrats of Taunton Vale (Grantham being two centuries older). Louth's steeple is also the tallest; at 295 ft it is 3 ft higher than St Mary Redcliffe, Bristol. It was built in 1501–15 by masons from Lincoln, and completed shortly before Lincolnshire's rebellion against the Reformation. Louth's vicar was to be executed at Tyburn, and much of the church's furnishing destroyed by iconoclasts.

The tower is a superb composition, the upward line perfectly modulated by horizontal divisions. The deep west doorway projects forward of the west front, its ogee gable carried up to the level of the west window. This window rises to a pair of windows and then to paired openings for the bell-chamber with more ogees. Finally we reach the astonishing enrichment of the battlements. The pinnacles are 50 ft high, readying the eye for a spire supported by open flying buttresses. This soars on upwards, its mason even spacing the crockets more widely as the apex approaches, thus syncopating the perspective. Not an element is out of place. The work is in every way a match for the contemporary Renaissance architecture of southern Europe.

The interior of Louth is almost domestic in comparison, 'friendlier than Boston' asserts the verger. The tower arch reflects the splendour of its exterior. Inside the tower a 'starburst' vault is set above the windows, creating a magnificent lantern. Below is surely the most spectacularly roofed coffee bar in England.

The rest of the interior was heavily treated in the 19th century but more sensitively by the 20th. The nave is dominated by its late Georgian pine roof, a magnificent composition of tie-beams and panels, restored in 1988 by Richard Benny of Lincoln. He stripped the wood and repainted the angels in red and blue. The corbel heads supporting the wall-posts are original, and stare out like monsters on the congregation below.

The south chapel contains beautiful Decorated sedilia, while fixed to the wall of the north chapel are two medieval angels rescued from the former roof and here visible at close quarters. Louth has a superb collection of old 'hutches' or chests. Most date from the Middle Ages, but my favourite is a 20th-century work with swirling neo-Gothic patterns in the side panels.

Norfolk

King's Lynn

ST MARGARET
Norman west front, chancel carvings,
'peacock feast' brass

Poor King's Lynn, so dreadfully treated by the 20th century, still has corners of delight. Like most such corners, this one surrounds its church. St Margaret's remains the glory of the town, over which its twin towers stand like guardian angels. Despite the loss of the south-west spire, which crashed into the nave during a storm in 1741, and despite the bashings of every age, the church is a place of urban dignity. In the words of its excellent guide, its 'sturdy, muddled architecture has no claim to elegance'. Yet the church offers a stately progression, from Norman walling in the west front to Victorian reredos, that includes work of every period.

The church was founded (with Great Yarmouth) by Bishop Losinga of Norwich in 1101, as penance for his corruption in buying the See. The town was called Bishop's Lynn until after the Reformation and is just Lynn to its inhabitants. The church setting is 'town', with buildings huddled close on all sides. The two west towers rise above cliffs of Norman masonry, embedded in additions that appear to have no feature in common.

This diversity is even more evident inside the west entrance. Norman wall shafting, like corrugation, continues round the tower supports. That on the north side leans markedly, as a result of medieval subsidence. The shafting on the south encloses a wall passage large enough to belong to a cathedral.

The nave is 18th-century Perpendicular, built by Matthew Brettingham of Holkham after the tower collapse. The charm of the interior lies east, in the 13th-century crossing and chancel. The piers have stiff-leaf on every capital. The arcades here form a gallery of medieval sculpture, a strip cartoon of Lynn's domestic life. A demon hugs a man, a woman is trapped in a scold's bridle and there are Green Men aplenty. The restored east window is a huge composition, a rose formed of Panel tracery. This was reconstructed in the 1870s from fragments found on the site and is somewhat tenuously claimed as the 'biggest Perpendicular rose in England'. The cheap painted glass is an insult and should be removed. The window forms a halo above Bodley's golden reredos of 1899. This is a masterpiece, with Christ blessing Gregory, Jerome, Augustine and Ambrose above beautiful reliefs of Bible scenes.

St Margaret's is a forest of screens and stalls. The former are mostly pre-Perpendicular, a rare display in wood of such Decorated motifs as steep gables, sharply pointed arches, trefoils, and ogees both flat and nodding. In among them are faces replicating those on the walls above. The misericords are excellent. The 16th-century eagle lectern once had its beak open to receive Peter's Pence, but this was later closed. Elizabethan screens shield the organ, its case a spectacular rococo work of 1754. The organist at the time was Dr Burney, father of Fanny and friend of Mozart.

The church's other treasures are the brasses in the south aisle. They are of Adam de Walsoken and Robert Braunche, of 1349 and 1364 respectively, among the largest and most elaborate brasses anywhere and normally credited to Flemish artists working in Bruges. While the faces and canopies are stylised, the clothes and panels appear to be specific to their subjects. The magnates of medieval Lynn were men of business and politics, not war. Under Braunche's feet is a depiction of a celebrated feast of peacocks he staged for Edward III in 1349.

Salle

ST PETER AND ST PAUL
Norfolk's rural cathedral, font cover,
carved bosses and choir stalls

Salle is a favourite of Norfolk church enthusiasts, isolated, wild and vast. Pronounced Saul, it booms out to travellers across the north Norfolk plain like an architectural foghorn. Its tower was erected on the wealth of wool and is now sustained on the love of its group of loyal parishioners. Salle might be a church of the Castilian plain, enriched with the gold of the Americas and far beyond the means or needs of its community. It is as much a testament to economic history as to faith.

The church was rebuilt in the early 15th century, paid for by Uffords, Mautebys, Morleys and Brewes. Rather than use cheap local flint, they brought costly Barnack stone from Peterborough, and were duly blessed for their generosity with two feathered angels waving censers over their coats of arms above the west door. By the middle of the century they had been joined by another cloth tycoon, Everard Brigg, whose E is worked into the tower parapet. The south transept was built by the St James's Guild, with the letter T for Thomas Brigg on its facade. The Brigg arms are also above the central niche of the south porch. The porches at Salle are big and double-storeyed.

Now for the inside. Entry is by the west door and the spectacle from the entrance is superb. The nave is as calm as the fields outside. Arcades rise and fall towards the chancel arch. An interior of immense height and volume frames the crockets of an elegant font cover. This is suspended from a huge bracket projecting from the bell-ringers' gallery in the tower, both embellished with tracery. Beneath this cover rests one of the best Seven-Sacrament fonts in Norfolk, its panels excellently preserved. Beneath each scene is a small angel holding the symbol of the sacrament above, such as the scourge as symbol of penance.

The roofs are no less splendid. The nave has a plain arch-brace with angels at the junctions of the rafters. The shallow transept roofs have charming cusped panels, while that of the St James's Guild Chapel in the south transept is allegedly the original for the roof of the House of Lords. Finest of all is the chancel roof, lifted into the sky on the wings of 160 angels, punctuated by a set of carved bosses worthy of any cathedral. Since they are near-invisible, there is a helpful photographic display of them on the wall. They show scenes from the Life of Christ, each ingeniously fitted into a circle. In a most explicit Circumcision, the baby seeks Mary's breast for comfort.

The nave contains a contemporary 15th-century wine-glass pulpit, painted red and green, fashioned into a three-decker by a 17th-century clerk's desk and a reading desk. The furnishings include original choir stalls and misericords. The arm-rests and seats are a gallery of 15th-century vernacular art: dolphins, swans, squirrels, dragons and the heads of Green Men, all peering from flowers, fruit and leaves of familiar trees. The chancel also retains much original glass. On the north side are portrayals of patriarchs and even three cardinals in wide hats. They must have done well to survive the Reform-ation. The main east window glass is fragmentary but includes some vivid colouring, including pieces of dragons' wings.

A door in the north-west corner of the church gives access to the parvise of a porch. This was variously a priest's home, chapel and schoolroom. It has superb coloured bosses. The view from its window over the Norfolk countryside on a clear winter evening is one of utter tranquillity.

Walpole St Peter

Nave woodwork, font cover, 'bolt-hole' tunnel

The 'Queen of the Marshlands' deserves more respect than she has been accorded. The Walpoles may be safe from flooding, but are inundated by bungalow estates.

St Peter's is to west Norfolk what Salle is to the east, a church for the connoisseur of this noble county. It is a place not of curiosity but of subtle proportion, of the play of light on stone and wood. If English churches were Dutch Old Masters, this would be St Pieter de Hooch.

The exterior is supremely graceful, early Perpendicular of *c.*1400, with ogees still in some of the window tracery. Wherever we look there is decoration, on the buttresses, the string courses, the battlements, even the sanctus bellcote, the last a gem of Gothic detailing. The porch is sumptuous, of two bays and two storeys. This is stone vaulted with a full set of bosses, each a meticulous example of 15th-century carving. The Perpendicular oak door is original. A sign warns worshippers to remove their pattens, or wooden shoes, before entering, with an old pair hanging by the door to illustrate the point.

Inside there is hardly a disappointment. We are met by a font with nodding ogees round its base and a Jacobean cover. Its fretwork rises like some exotic Ottoman smoking machine. The rear of the nave is enclosed by a 17th-century screen running the width of the building. This has three pediments and turns the rear of the nave into a foyer, as if guarding the entrance to a theatre. The nave arcades are early Perpendicular – the guide even hazards 'Transitional-Perpendicular' as if eager to invent a 14th-century style of its own – with piers shafted and arches steeply pointed. They hold the key to the charm of this church. Within its Perpendicular embrace survives the form of an earlier, more mobile Gothic of the decades before the Black Death.

The roof is surprisingly simple, with no decoration

above the corbel level, but with a huge chandelier of 1701. Beneath is spread a carpet of light oak furniture. The pews date from the 15th to the 17th centuries and are enriched throughout. Those in the south aisle face laterally into the nave, rising in three tiers, as if meant for schoolchildren. Overlooking this array is a high pulpit on a spindly stem with tester above. The nave is completed by two aisle chapels, with a coloured Perpendicular screen in the south one. St Peter's has a rare 'hudd', or portable cubicle to protect the priest from rain when conducting burials before the invention of umbrellas.

The chancel is marked only by the dado of an old screen, still with painted panels. On either side are two doors to the vanished rood loft, both immaculate Decorated compositions with ogee arches. The chancel sanctuary eventually rises a total of 24 steps from the nave, granting it an overpowering presence. This has blind arcading, forming sedilia where appropriate. Each bay has tiny imitation rib vaults in its canopy. The corner niches are crowned with dogs. The saints' niches on the walls have lovely nodding ogee canopies.

Finally there is the tunnel. This is not just a 'bolt hole', its local nickname, but a passage with cobbles underfoot, tierceron vault and no fewer than 12 bosses. It must form the handsomest covered street in England. The purpose is unknown, but it was probably an ancient processional route of such significance that nobody dared divert it when the chancel was rebuilt above. Next to the church is the yew hedge of the old rectory, with a tree clipped into the shape of a cross.

Northamptonshire

Lowick

ST PETER
Octagonal tower, medieval glass, Greene effigies

Lowick church is a hidden masterpiece of English Perpendicular. Its village lies off the beaten track south of Oundle, and the church is detached even from the village, alone in a field. The tower with its octagonal top stage is visible for miles around, a forest of pinnacles topped by golden weathervanes. From a distance they seem to flutter in the sun, like pennants summoning us to some forgotten Tudor tournament. By the time of the tower's completion, in the 1470s, octagons were in fashion in these parts, as at neighbouring Fotheringhay.

The church was built by the Greene family, of the adjacent Drayton House. They built sumptuously. As we climb up the hill from the south-east, we are presented with a lavish 15th-century chancel and chapel, with Panel tracery in the large windows, that have to be supported by heavy buttresses. Inside, all is light. The architecture is conventional Perpendicular. A large coat of arms crowns the chancel arch and a Victorian screen bars the transept chapel. The sedilia, with lovely ogee arches, must have been retrieved from an earlier church.

But these are preliminaries to Lowick's treasures, its medieval glass and its monuments.

The glass is in the upper half of the north aisle windows. It runs along the length of the aisle, an orderly progression of the most vivid colour. How it survived the iconoclasts is a mystery. The narrative is of the Tree of Jesse, showing the Old Testament origins of Jesus. In the right-hand window can be seen a knight holding a church, presumably an early donor. The windows have been dated to the 1320s and were thus, like the sedilia, reset in the new church.

The monuments form a familiar contrast of medieval serenity and Georgian bombast. Between the north-east chapel and the nave lie Ralph Greene (d.1417) and his wife. This is one of the finest alabaster tombs in England. The effigy dates from the creative burst in English art at the turn of the 15th century and is the only one in existence for which a contract survives. This is from Greene's wife to two Derbyshire carvers named Thomas Prentys and Robert Sutton, for 'a counterfeit of an esquire all armed for battle'. The pair lie in effigy with tiny lierne-vaulted canopies above their heads. Her head-dress and coat illustrate the wilder shores of contemporary fashion. He wears chainmail and armour but has removed his gauntlet to hold his wife's hand in death. The work is stiff yet moving.

We now move to the south chapel. In the centre lies a monument to Edward, Earl of Wiltshire, who died in 1499 and was a Greene grandson. Again the effigy is of the highest quality. The knight wears a Lancastrian 'SS' collar and has tiny bedesmen under his feet. Opposite is an extraordinary Westmacott monument of 1843 to the Duke of Dorset. A white tomb chest carries not an effigy or even medallion but the duke's cloak, shield and coronet, with an angel holding a text. The title became extinct with his death, so perhaps the iconography is appropriate. In the north-east chapel we find a cosy group of Lady Mordaunt (d.1705) resting on a skull. She lies with her second husband, Sir John Germain, who is in old-fashioned armour with his legs in an awkward pose.

Stanford on Avon

ST NICHOLAS
Stone and wood carving, medieval glass,
Cave monuments

This superb church lies to the east of the William-and-Mary Stanford Hall, a house designed by Smith of Warwick. It has been home of the Caves and their descendants, the Brayes, to this day and their monuments fill the church. The churchyard is a meadow whose gate firmly warns us to keep out the sheep. The windows alternate graceful Intersecting and a swaying Reticulated tracery. The steeple lacks a spire, the crude tower pinnacles forming a sort of apology.

The interior is mostly clear of pews. With the chancel, it offers a gallery of church furnishing, glass and sculpture as complete as that of any small parish church. The nave arcades are limestone arches with no capitals, just a continuous, sweeping arc. The stone carvers were confined to the spandrels. Others were at work round the south aisle piscina and others still on the Decorated font.

Stanford is rich in woodwork. The chancel roof beams are apparently Norman in origin, while the dark oak wall panelling is 16th century, from the former Stanford Hall. The sanctuary chairs are Flemish, their backs portraying Stations of the Cross, and the altar was that used by William Laud, vicar here in 1607 before his ascent to Canterbury. Gnarled choir stalls display poppyheads and misericords. Indeed all the furnishings are pre-Victorian. Even the church doors have medieval woodwork. The organ case in the west gallery is Tudor, said to have been removed by Cromwell from Whitehall Palace after the execution of Charles I and acquired by Thomas Cave. How many such treasures are dispersed unrecorded in England's parish churches?

The Stanford monuments commemorate generations of Caves, a parade of gentry from the Middle Ages to the 19th century, courtiers, soldiers, priests, scholars, custodians of the heart of England. There are 15 tombs scattered round the church with an enjoyable juxtaposition of styles. Nothing charts the changes in English taste over the centuries so much as funerary sculpture. From wealth and pomposity to misery, piety and gloom, Stanford recalls it all.

The monuments are in a chronological jumble, and the more delightful for that. In the south aisle, the tomb of the medieval priest who built the church (Alan de Aslaghby) lies under a fine Decorated recess. Against the west wall is a mid-Victorian marble monument to Sarah, Baroness Braye (d.1862), by Mary Thornycroft. The effigy lies asleep with dead lilies in her hand. A friend watches over her, while her children are angels in the sky. She herself gathered the coloured stones from Italy that form the paving before her tomb.

Across the nave on the north-west wall is another large Victorian piece, by Westmacott. Robert Otway Cave (d.1844) sleeps with his head affectedly on his hand. A woman weeps as she inscribes his praises, his books lying dishevelled by his side. Next is an extraordinary memorial by Felix Joubert of 1896, to Edmund Verney who fell in the Zulu wars. Next door are the recumbent effigies of Margaret Cave and her husband (*c.*1600) lying as if on shelves, one above the other.

The chancel monuments include a panel to Thomas Otway Cave (d.1830), in which piety and pain are on full display. His wife weeps while an angel cruelly extinguishes a huge torch in the earth. A fine Jacobean monument in red-streaked marble next to the sanctuary celebrates Sir Thomas Cave (d.1613). It is oddly linked by a scroll to a cenotaph to his eldest son Richard, who died on a visit to Italy at the age of nineteen. He was clearly much favoured.

I cannot write of Stanford's glass, reputedly the best in the county, as it was being restored during my visit. Photographs inside the south door show that it includes early 14th-century as well as later heraldic windows. Among the former is a rare depiction of the Virgin, most such depictions being destroyed by iconoclasts. Stanford retains a fine collection of cobwebs. The habitat of the noble spider is, like the stones themselves, a symbol of the passage of time.

Wellingborough

ST MARY, KNOX ROAD
Comper's masterpiece interior

The church lies along the eastern skyline of Welling-borough near the station. Here in a suburb of a lifeless Midlands town is the masterpiece of Sir Ninian Comper and one of the most splendid large church interiors of the 20th century. It is well supported and in good hands, but there can be few such unknown and unobtrusive monuments in this book.

Comper regarded St Mary's as his favourite church and wished to be buried here with his wife, though a grateful nation sent him finally to Westminster Abbey. The church was begun in 1908 under the patronage of the spinster Misses Sharman, daughters of a local landowner. It did not reach its present state until the 1950s. The plan is simple Perpendicular with transepts and full-length aisles, based on St Patrice in Rouen. The exterior is uninteresting.

The north-west door opens to a waft of incense, for the church has always been Anglo-Catholic. The first impression is sensational, intended, in Betjeman's words, 'to force even the atheist to his knees'. The interior is crowded with the inspiration of European Gothicism down the ages. The volume is vast, filled with waving fan vaults and dripping pendants above a sumptuous golden sanctuary, a sort of fantastical King's College Chapel, Cambridge.

The nave has eight bays of ironstone piers with concave sides, as at Northleach (Gloucs), and unorthodox capitals of Comper's own design. The painted roof decoration was never completed. Over the rood screen can be seen the black-and-white paint scheme intended for the arcade, while the western nave bays show the blue-and-gold paint intended for the vault. Finishing both should be a challenge to any conservationist.

Moving eastwards, the inspiration is increasingly Italianate. The rood screen has gilded Doric columns and exquisitely decorated spandrels and loft. It is surmounted by golden angels each with six folded wings and crowned above with a Christ in Majesty, based on the Christ Pantokrator in the apse of the Capella Palatina in Palermo. It is, said Comper, 'as much Italian as English and English as Italian'. The intricate ironwork of the screen is repeated in the filigree patterning round the north chapel.

The sanctuary is protected by a palisade of screens, angels, bridges and painted surfaces. The altar shelters under a ciborium with gilded Corinthian columns, crowned by cherubs and a Resurrection. They are brought forward into the church in the manner of San Clemente in Rome. The font is magnificent, surrounded by an octagonal screen with gilded dolphins. Of other furnishings there are few. The thin pulpit seems to disapprove of anyone preaching in such a church.

The interior of St Mary's has a remarkable completeness. Not every critic has liked it. Comper had his detractors and the vicar's bitter opposition to the eclectic nature of the fittings led Comper to resign twice during construction. But even Pevsner, ultra-Modernist in his taste for 20th-century architecture, was won over. He wrote that St Mary's 'glistens and reveals and conceals to one's heart's delight'. Its day has yet to come.

Northumberland

Hexham

PRIORY
Saxon crypt, canons' night staircase, 'Dance of Death'

This splendid church asserts itself uncompromisingly in the centre of the old fortress town, presenting its gate and walls to the market square. In the Middle Ages this was turbulent country. The 7th-century foundation by St Wilfrid was plundered and burnt by the Vikings. It was refounded in 1113 as an Augustinian priory but attacked by the Scots under William Wallace at the end of the 13th century, when the nave was destroyed and not rebuilt.

After the Dissolution the citizens used the chancel as a church. The eastern bay of the chancel collapsed in the 19th century and a road was then driven through the monastic ruins. It was not until 1905 that thought and money were given to building a proper nave and restoring dignity to the composition. The priory buildings have long gone.

The architect of the new work, which included both a nave and a new east wall facing the market, was Temple Moore. He apparently used the Decorated style so as not to appear to be copying anything in the original church. The result is really two contrasting churches at Hexham, the old church to the east comprising the magnificent crossing and chancel, and Moore's rather cold and scholastic nave to the west.

The east end of Hexham is the apotheosis of Early Gothic in a parish church. We enter it as the canons would have done, by a passage known as a slype at the end of the south transept. It linked the church with the monastic buildings to the south. The entrance thus gives directly onto the interior in the most dramatic possible fashion. The transept is dominated by the priory's famous night staircase, once leading directly to the canons' dormitory from which they could troop down for nocturnal services. This is one of the finest monastic relics in an English church. Above this stage rise two tiers of superb lancets: the lower tier is plain with blind arcading, the upper is fenestrated with rich shafts and mouldings. They form a wonderful group, a completely developed Gothic that would make a perfect set for a medieval film. Above both transepts are 15th-century roofs with bosses intact.

The view east from the crossing is dominated by the chancel arch. Beneath is a complete 16th-century screen and rood loft. It is the work of one of the last priors, Master Thomas Smithson, whose term ended just before the Dissolution in 1524. The dado panels still carry paintings of saints and bishops of Hexham and Lindisfarne. Also on the screen are a Visitation and a poignant Annunciation. On a wall of the sanctuary is another remarkable survival of medieval art, a 'Dance of Death', the best preserved in England. Centrepiece of the choir is the frith stool, or bishop's throne, one of only two dating from the Saxon period and carved from a single block of stone. Frith means peace, and the stool symbolises Wilfrid's right to grant sanctuary up to a mile from the seat. This right was abolished in 1624.

In the north choir aisle is the chantry chapel of Prior Leschman, Smithson's predecessor who died in 1491. The chamber is guarded by a crude figure believed to be St Christopher. The prior's tomb chest is adorned with stone carvings which, as Pevsner comments, are barbaric and 'surprisingly inappropriate for their purpose'. Some are of almost Aztec primitiveness and ferocity. One is of a fox preaching to geese, familiar satire on the clergy, but why on a prior's tomb? The effigy of the prior is abstract and has, most unusually, his cowl drawn down over his eyes.

Temple Moore's nave is handsome rather than moving. Even the best 20th-century architecture cannot recreate the mystery of the Middle Ages. Beneath it is the old Saxon crypt, a tunnel-vaulted chamber built partly of Roman stones with carved ornaments and inscriptions. Its arch reputedly dates from the 7th century. Like all such small places, Hexham crypt has a remarkable power of calm.

The church possesses many relics of Celtic and Roman occupation. In the south transept is the tombstone of a Roman soldier, Flavinus, riding his horse above a cowering British native. He was twenty-five years old and had seen seven years' service in these parts. Hexham is admirably lit.

Nottinghamshire

Clumber

ST MARY
Bodley's neo-Gothic masterpiece

The descendants of Bess of Hardwick created the Dukeries, a belt of architectural magnificence east of Hardwick in the environs of Sherwood Forest. Their descendants mostly destroyed that magnificence. The seat of the Dukes of Newcastle, Clumber House, was demolished between the two world wars. The majestic park remains in the care of the National Trust and contains the finest avenues in the Midlands.

Nobody had the courage to demolish the church. It was commissioned by the delicate and devout Anglo-Catholic 7th Duke, nephew of the patron of All Saints, Margaret Street in London and patron of Comper's work at Egmanton. On his own estate he determined to give Bodley free rein, at the then huge cost of £30,000. The duke was just twenty-two at the time of the commission in 1886, Bodley was sixty. They eventually quarrelled over Bodley's expenditure (which rose to £40,000) and the work was completed by others, but Bodley continued to regard Clumber as his finest creation.

The plan of the church is symmetrical and cruciform. The exterior soars upwards, the nave windows are set high, and the tower turns octagonal before ascending as a spire. The model is Patrington (Yorks, ER). The stone is white which, according to Bodley, 're-echoes the silvery gleam of the cold English sky', with red Runcorn sandstone dressings. Seen from the south down by the lake, Clumber Chapel is a truly spectacular work of art.

The Runcorn stone used sparingly outside is used throughout the interior, warm and rich when lit by sun or candlelight. The nave is handsome but austere, the duke separating his estate workers from the majesty of the Mass beyond the chancel screen. The chancel is almost as long as the nave, and considerably grander, flanked by side chapels. Its stalls were designed and carved by Ernest Geldart, a priest and craftsman who completed the furnishing of the church after the duke had fallen out with Bodley. (Geldart also designed the astonishing Hispanic reredos at St Cuthbert, Philbeach Gardens, in London.) But Bodley had time to design the pulpit, lectern and superb screen with intricate Perpendicular tracery. His too is the organ case, at a giddy height above the chancel.

Contract for the stained glass at Clumber went to Kempe, favoured artist (over Morris) of the Anglo-Catholic movement. The church contains some of his most refined work. The east window is a Crucifixion, surrounded by the works of Christ and, below, a depiction of Adam and Eve copied from Dürer. Its architectural detail mirrors that of the niches and canopies that fill the sanctuary. The west window is a Tree of Jesse.

The north transept contains a classical monument by Westmacott to Georgiana, wife of the 4th Duke.

The Regency style, complete with angelic messengers, would, as the guidebook says, 'have astonished and dismayed' the 7th Duke.

Newark-on-Trent

ST MARY
Decorated tower and civic nave,
Dance of Death painting

Newark and Grantham still soar over the east Midlands as they did in the Middle Ages. Grantham may have the finer steeple, but Newark outclasses it as a medieval church. Built over the two centuries of Perpendicular ascendancy after the Black Death, it piles high above its constricted urban site. A style so often dull is here exhilarating, the vistas majestic, the furnishings rich. As the country towns of England emerge from relative depression, these vast churches must revive as centres of cultural and civic activity.

The plan to rebuild the former church took shape in 1310. It began with the completion of the old Early Gothic tower and south aisle in the prevailing Decorated style. The tower thus starts at the bottom with 13th-century blind arcading and trelliswork – but with a Perpendicular window inserted. It rises to Decorated bell-openings under a crocketed gable. The parapet barely interrupts the broaching, as square turns to octagon at the foot of the spire. This spire soars to 236 ft, 50 ft shorter than Grantham.

The rest of the church was not finished until the early 16th century. By then Newark boasted sixteen guild and chantry chapels, two of which survive either side of the high altar. Though battered by Reformation and Civil War, Newark was not as altered in the 19th century as was Grantham. The walls are unscraped, apart from a patch above the chancel arch, and the roofs gloriously painted. The north side windows are mostly clear but the heavy colouring of the south windows is a blight, despite fine pieces by both Kempe and Wailes.

The nave is a wonder of proportion. Pevsner attributes this to the old Decorated plan, giving the aisles breadth, while the later masons added height. The vista thus extends horizontally and vertically. The chancel is marked by a fine Perpendicular screen and contemporary stalls and misericords. Glowing at its heart is a Comper masterpiece, a reredos of 1937, commissioned to cover a 19th-century one. On either side are the surviving chantries, now rather bare. Outside the south chantry is a fragment of a medieval Dance of Death, once so frequent in English churches but now rare. The panel carries the familiar warning, 'As I am today, so you will be tomorrow.'

The Lady Chapel contains a row of 15th-century sedilia above which the Victorians placed a mosaic of Van Eyck's *Adoration of the Lamb*. The east window of the Holy Spirit Chapel brings together Newark's surviving medieval glass in a composition of Old and New Testament stories. Next to it rises John Hardman's vast memorial east window to Prince Albert. The northern chapel is dedicated to the Sherwood Foresters regiment and is decorated by Caröe.

Back in the nave, Newark's font was desecrated by

iconoclasts. The base is medieval while the bowl is of 1660, with Cavalier heads in a classical setting. Next to it is the Markham monument of 1601. Anne Markham is pictured surrounded by her children under a knot of drapery, set in the purest of classical frames.

Oxfordshire

Bloxham

ST MARY
Window carvings, Milcombe Chapel, Burne-Jones glass

Bloxham is a steeple, a window and a chapel. The steeple is a work of art in itself, early 14th century and the finest in Oxfordshire. Bloxham church, with its adjacent school, enjoyed royal patronage until the Dissolution, when it passed to Eton College. The octagon and spire rise 200 ft, almost sheer from the road.

Every surface of the tower is carved. Below the parapet is a frieze of men and beasts, which continues along the north aisle and recalls similar work at Adderbury. The west doorway arch has carvings of the apostles in small niches, with a Last Judgment at the apex. The masons seem to have usurped all convention and set free their imaginations. The brown marlestone is badly eroded, in part by its proximity to the main road, and some carvings are Victorian replicas. In which case, I cannot see what is served by letting the others crumble to nothing. New ones should surely take their place, true to the Victorian practice. If the statues at Chartres can be replaced, why not at Bloxham?

The inside of the church is not easy to read: essentially a 14th-century Decorated structure encasing Norman and Early Gothic features, but with spectacular additions in the Perpendicular period. The south doorway is part-Norman. The nave arcades are Early Gothic, the stone dark and often undressed. The double arch that divides the north aisle from the transept has a superb capital adorned with heads, arms and shields. Most remarkable of the windows is that at the west end of the north aisle, where the tracery is carved with figures both inside and out. This rare practice, also found at Dorchester, must have been intended to complement the story told in the window glass. It here illustrates the Bible in a stone wheel with Christ at its hub.

Roughly a century later came a burst of Perpendicular patronage, probably from the hand of the same Richard Winchcombe as worked at Adderbury. If so, to him we owe the three great windows inserted in the east end of the aisles, and the Milcombe Chapel, a classic of early 15th century Perpendicular. The contrast with the chancel east window and with the rest of the building is complete. Areas of Panel tracery support large expanses of clear glass. Mullions soar from floor to ceiling. Light floods in past the delicate concave piers of the arcade, like a conservatory tacked onto a gloomy stately home. The chapel was later taken over by the Thornycroft family and contains a number of their monuments. Sir John Thornycroft (d.1725) lies in effigy, smug with his books, as if this room had been built for his personal and eternal use.

The last phase of Bloxham's development came with Street's restoration and the employment of Morris & Co for the glass. The chancel interior is largely Street, as are the pulpit, choir stalls and marble reredos. The chancel east window glass is an early masterpiece by Morris, Burne-Jones and Webb. It depicts saints, angels and King Alfred set before the Heavenly City. The colours are bold and the effect dramatic. Even more lovely is the vividly coloured window of St Christopher in the south wall of the chancel. It was executed in 1920 to a Burne-Jones design.

Burford

ST JOHN
Merchants' guild chapel, Red Indian memorial,
Kempe glass

Burford is queen of Oxfordshire, a paragon and museum of the English parish church. It stands where the Thames basin folds into the Cotswolds. Here wealthy medieval cloth merchants exchanged bills of trading, and poured much of the profit into God's House. The spire can be seen rising over the little town from along the Windrush valley, yet it contrives to vanish from within the town, to be found hidden down a lane at the foot of the High Street.

The charm of Burford church lies in personal rather than civic ostentation. No consortium of patrons was ever gathered to rebuild it afresh, as in most wool towns of the Cotswolds and East Anglia. The church is thus a work of accretion. Chapels were added when persons or guilds so decided. The tower is a Norman survival, as is the west door. The panelled and pinnacled entrance porch has three storeys of chambers, almost as grand as that at Cirencester (Gloucs), and modern statues in its niches. To its left runs the Guild of Merchants Chapel, erected *c.*1200 as a separate building. It was remodelled and joined to the main structure in the late 15th century.

Burford's interior is a maze of low arches, surprising vistas, chapels and shrines. The church counted nine separate altars and six incumbent priests at the start of the 16th century. After the Reformation, the chapels and chantries were converted for use as family pews and mausoleums. St Thomas's Chapel, between the south transept and porch, became the Corporation Pew. The chantry chapel in the north aisle became the Lord of the Manor's Pew. The large Guild of Merchants Chapel became the resting place for the Sylvesters, among the richest of Burford's 16th-century merchants. The last Sylvester commemorated here died in 1904.

In the nave north aisle, a superb classical memorial recalls Edmund Harman (d.1569), Henry VIII's barber and courtier. Harman married a Sylvester after acquiring the local Hospital of St John after the Dissolution. His memorial, completed before his death, carries the first known depiction in England of the Indian inhabitants of the New World, believed to have been copied from a Flemish book. The connection with Harman is unknown, though the intention was probably to indicate the cosmopolitan reach of the town's trade. Spotlit on the turret wall opposite the south transept chapel is a primitive carved panel dated *c.*160 AD. It is of three figures and a horse, said to allude to the Celtic fertility goddess Epona. Alternatively it may be a Flight into Egypt or Christ's Entry into Jerusalem, surviving from a Saxon church.

The north chancel chapel contains the celebrated Tan-field monument, erected by the wife of Sir Lawrence Tanfield, a prominent judge, in 1628. The couple were unpopular in Burford and, on Tanfield's death, the church refused his widow permission for a memorial, one having already been refused at Westminster Abbey. She was adamant that her husband should have a tomb appropriate to his status, and marched her workmen in undaunted. They erected six Corinthian columns, arches, obelisks and the Tanfield coat of arms above effigies of the couple lying in prayer. For good measure, Lady Tanfield added her own verse. 'So shall I be / With him I loved / And he with me / And both us blessed. / Love made me poet / And this I writt. / My harte did doe it / And not my witt.' The church let them be.

Burford was later the scene of greater strife. In May 1649 Cromwell imprisoned a group of Leveller mutineers in the church for three nights, after which they were to be shot. When three had been executed, Cromwell relented and forced the rest to submit to a recanting sermon by their own leader. One of the prisoners, Anthony Sedley, scratched his name on the font. A more drastic assault on the church came in the 19th century with its restoration by Street. After he had already rebuilt the chancel roof, William Morris arrived from nearby Kelmscott to protest. The vicar, W. A. Cass, retorted: 'The church, Sir, is mine and if I choose to, I shall stand on my head in it.' The infuriated Morris later founded the Society for the Protection of Ancient Buildings.

That said, the vicar, or perhaps the architect, was sufficiently moved to refrain from meddling with the nave. The roof was retained but the manorial pew was restored as a chapel of St Peter. Nor could Morris have objected to the use of the young Charles Kempe for the glass in eight of Burford's windows. The west window installed in 1869 portrays the Tree of Jesse and incorporates medieval fragments. It is full of the colours, animated figures and foliage of the Pre-Raphaelite school. Facing it above the crossing arch is a large painted Crucifixion by Clayton & Bell in the style of Piero della Francesca.

The churchyard has a set of bale-tombs almost as good as those at Painswick (Gloucs). These stone chests of about 1700 are topped by 'bales', possibly representing cloth, and carved with cherubs and skulls. They crowd the path like a congregation discussing the sermon after church.

Dorchester

ABBEY OF ST PETER AND ST PAUL
Carved window tracery, lead font,
'action effigy' of knight

Dorchester was once a capital of England. Its writ ran north to the Humber, even to Northumbria. St Birinus brought Christianity here and founded a cathedral in the 7th century. But the See departed first for Winchester and then for Lincoln, leaving Dorchester as an abbey. The church is set on a curving high street next to the juvenile Thames, still surrounded by fragments of the medieval abbey which are buried in walls and poke up through shrubbery.

The first impression of the interior is gloomy. We

enter through the south nave aisle, added *c.*1340 for use as a parish church. Its altar had to be raised and set off-centre, above a burial vault for graves disturbed during the building. A large faded wall painting survives. The aisle is enlivened by a variety of sculpture. A Norman lead font is decorated with eleven apostles. They are either minus Judas or, since one appears to be Christ, also minus Doubting Thomas. Lead was used to avoid holy water escaping by seeping through the stone. Such fonts are rare. The designs have been traced to workshops in the Bristol area, possibly under the influence of Carolingian craftsmen in Germany. On a nearby corbel, attached to one of the arcade piers, a devil blows his horn to awaken the canons to service.

The celebrated 'action effigy' of an unknown knight in the south aisle dates from *c.*1280. The figure is portrayed in the act of drawing his sword, his back and limbs contorted into life. The sculptor seems struggling to escape the stone, to transmit some urgent message.

Shropshire

Shrewsbury

ST MARY
Norman Transitional arcades, medieval glass

Since its rescue by the Churches Conservation Trust and the restoration of its glass, St Mary's has re-emerged as one of the great churches of the Marches. Its 222-ft spire dominates the old part of the town and its architecture offers a full range of Norman and Gothic design. The stained glass is as remarkable as that of Ludlow or Great Malvern (Worcs).

The church holds court in an attractive close. The west tower wall carries a plaque commemorating a steeplejack named Robert Cadman who, in 1739, plunged to his death while walking a tightrope strung from the tower across the Severn to Gaye Meadow. The exterior of sandstone and ashlar is easily read, with Norman tower and porches, Early Gothic transepts with lancet windows, Perpendicular in the aisles and a large south-east chapel in the Decorated style.

The interior contrives to be both majestic and intimate. The nave is of the Transitional style, c.1200. The arcades display rounded (Norman) arches above (Early Gothic) shafted piers. The same period is evident in the capitals: Norman scallop and trumpet in the tower arch, the stiffest of stiff-leaf in the south arcade, and free Early Gothic stiff-leaf with peering heads in the north arcade. Above rises a magnificent panelled roof of *c.*1500, with giant fleurons as bosses and angels with musical instruments. To the east the chancel arch is pointed but with two Victorian twin-light openings above it, a splendid composition.

Proceeding east we reach the transepts, both of them Early Gothic with high lancets, but with earlier Norman work intruding everywhere. The splendid glass in the chancel's east window is one of the most complete Tree of Jesse windows in the country, albeit brought here after the collapse of old St Chad's in the 18th century.

This window dates from the high-point of the Decorated period, 1330–50. Newer glass has been added at the top and the sides but most is original and excellently restored. Jesse lies at the foot of the composition, his tree rising and encircling the characters of the Old and New Testaments. Below him is Edward III, flanked by the donor, Sir John de Charlton, and members of his family.

The remaining glass in the church is almost all from the collection acquired by a Victorian vicar of St Mary's, William Rowland (1828–52), from various churches on the Continent. The glass is of remarkable quality. The Trinity Chapel has two windows of 16th-century Belgian glass. In the north window of the chancel are 14 panels of the life of St Bernard from Altenberg Abbey, near Cologne. The aisles contain three 1479 windows from Trier Cathedral and delightful panels from the Netherlands.

All these are 15th and 16th century and sit far more happily in this architecture than would the Victorian glass in so many town churches. They combine biblical, mythical and domestic scenes, much as did the artists of the later Golden Age, the Dutch 17th century. To wander from one window to the next is to see scenes and faces that might be taken from Dürer, Hieronymus Bosch or Brueghel. This is Shrewsbury's Old Master gallery, set in glass.

Only in the east window of the Trinity Chapel does Rowland assert his own talent: its two side lights were designed by a local man, David Evans, while the centre light and wheel window are by Powell & Sons, superbly Art Nouveau in swirling lines of vivid blues and reds. At its foot is a depiction of the town.

Somerset

Crewkerne

ST BARTHOLOMEW
Perpendicular window tracery,
'clean and unclean' doors

Crewkerne church was rebuilt at the turn of the 16th century. It is a church of vistas and perspectives. From the high ground to the west we see an embattled minster rising proud from a frame of trees. The grand west front is symmetrical, with windows, octagonal turrets and low-pitched roofs, and with battlements in balance above a doorway of ogee arch and niches. This is attributed to William Smyth of Wells and is considered by Kenneth Wickham the best in the county. Yet the view from the north gate is quite different. Here a horizontal sequence of six-light windows reaches almost to the ground. To the north-east we see no fewer than seven right angles, as transept, chancel, chancel aisles and chapel jostle for wall space.

The window tracery of Crewkerne is among the most complex Perpendicular work of any church in England. The style, lacking the flamboyance of Decorated, is sometimes regarded as tedious, yet at Crewkerne it blossoms into ceaseless invention. Mullions rise and split and replicate and cusp, demanding a pullout section to themselves in the church's admirable guide. Even more exciting is the effect these great windows have on the interior spaces. The church is cruciform and the crossing forms a dark sanctuary, from which transepts and aisles seem to spin outwards in search of the light.

This plan has all the exhilaration of German High Baroque. The view diagonally from the south aisle is of a forest of piers through which, on a sunny day, the fall of light on Ham stone, whitewashed walls and oak roofs is incomparable. The short aisled nave is a square of three bays with a high wagon roof. Both transepts are deep, but the north fragments into chapels and secluded chambers of high windows, carved screens and altars. The corbel heads in the crossing include an excellent Green Man, gazing down as though he were the presiding genius of the place.

The north end of the north transept is the Woolminstone Chapel, after the home of the Merefield family, whose banner hangs here. Next to it, behind modern screens, is the children's chapel with a classical altar. The chancel is dominated by Victorian and 20th-century furnishings, with a Ham stone reredos of the Last Supper. On either side of the sanctuary are two doorways, once thought to represent the unclean to the left (with spandrels of pigs) and the cleansed to the right (with angels). However, the guide suggests that boars were the arms of the local Courtenay family, and the angels were just angels.

Dunster

ST GEORGE
Longest screen, cloister garden

The view of Dunster from the coast road is rightly praised. The castle on its rock and the church tower lie against a backdrop of deep green Exmoor combes. The tumbling contours might be those of a Dutch Renaissance painting. Within the town, the church is well hidden behind the swoop of the main high street. It was once part of a Benedictine priory, its red sandstone exterior expressing strength rather than elegance. To the north of the church is the former cloister garden, surely the most delightful church garden in England. It is reached from the north transept or from a side road by the priory dovecote, a secret place filled with summer flowers.

The church's plan is cruciform. Fragments of the Norman priory can be detected on the west face of the crossing arch and in a restored west door. This was the church founded by William de Mohun, courtier of the Conqueror, as a gift to the monks of Bath. He was, he said, 'pricked by the fear of God'. There is no evidence that the great church planned by the monks with this gift ever extended beyond the present crossing.

The rest of the present church is Perpendicular, the divide between the monastic and civic church being the cause of lengthy litigation. The feud, typical of many churches at the end of the Middle Ages, pitted a distant monastic authority and its local agent, the prior, against an increasingly prosperous and assertive town. At one point the townspeople imprisoned the monks in the east end of the church. A settlement in 1498 found largely in favour of the parish.

The church was then split in two, a division clearly visible today. The townspeople constructed a long rood screen across the nave, three bays west of the crossing, to demarcate their own space. By then, they had crammed their own tower on top of the monks' Norman one, and completely surrounded the monastic chancel with aisles, transepts and chapels. They even tied up the bell-ropes so the monks could not sound their services. The screen which the town constructed is one of the finest in the West Country and reputedly the longest in England – or 'anywhere' hazards the guide. It is of 15 bays and stretches across the entire interior, nave and aisles. A choir can still allegedly perform on top. The bays between this screen and the crossing have choir stalls and candelabra, replacing the choir which was still occupied by the monks to the east.

Other screens have been reused to divide the chapels. The south transept chapel has part of the original rood screen, of superlative quality. The archway, seen down the south aisle, has a curious double curved arch, apparently the result of a remodelling to enable monks to process side by side. Behind are the monuments to the Luttrells, successors to the Mohuns as lords of Dunster from 1376. The one dedicated to George and Thomas, dating from 1613, is the only case I know of two couples sharing a single composition. Three of the four are recumbent, but George kneels behind his wife, presumably the last alive at the time. On the floor by the east wall is an incised alabaster memorial to Elizabeth Luttrell of 1493.

Dunster's chancel was 'authentically' restored by Street. The church has a fine collection of medieval muniment chests scattered about the aisles. In the tower is a carillon, one of the few examples in England of this delightful instrument.

Isle Abbotts

ST MARY
Taunton group tower, Perpendicular north aisle

Isle Abbotts is the monarch of the Somerset Levels. As Kenneth Wickham puts it, this remote moorland church 'sits like a queen with her court ranged around her in widening circles ... the heart and core of so much beauty'. The tower overlooks a tiny settlement on an isolated mound in the Levels north of Ilminster. It is attended by pretty thatched cottages, and less pretty council houses. The path to the porch runs deep through the vegetation of the churchyard. On my last visit roses and wild flowers were so abundant as almost to prevent access.

Ham stone did not come cheap. Like many churches Isle Abbotts used it only for decorating its tower, the structure itself being built of blue lias. The contrast between the two is softened by a patina of lichen. The tower is less ornate than Huish and Kingsbury Episcopi nearby, and virtually identical to the earlier Bishop's Lydeard and Kingston St Mary. Wickham attributes it to

the same designer or group of designers, variously called
the Quantock or Taunton group.

The tower's three stages are distinct, with each stage
framing windows and niches. Buttress pinnacles cling
close to the tower, pushing it upwards like rockets. The
rhythm of fenestration, the pierced battlements and the
delicacy of the crown render the structure light, almost
floating. No fewer than ten of the tower's original statues
survived the iconoclasts. The carving is as fine as the
St Andrew at High Ham. The Virgin has flowing hair.
The resurrected Christ rises from the tomb with figures
tumbling beneath Him. The hunky punks on the tower
summit are superb, including a man blowing a bagpipe.

This Somerset church has a body worthy of its head.
A walk round the north side reveals an aisle probably
added some forty years after the completion of the tower,
by that generous patron of late Gothic chapels, Lady
Margaret Beaufort. The south side of the church and the
chancel are a complete contrast to the north side. They
survive from the previous church of *c.*1300 and have
grouped and stepped lancets, and windows with Bar
tracery.

This contrast is reflected inside. The south wall is solid
and heavy and the eye is immediately led across the nave
to the glorious four-bay north arcade. Its piers have
capitals of foliage and the character of a theatrical pro-
scenium, framing the chapel beyond. On its stage, the
actors are beams of sunlight, playing across the warm
stone.

The chancel is no anticlimax. It is watched over by a
high pulpit and squint punched through the old rood

staircase. The piscina has a carved surround. The Norman font has flowers and monsters around its side. Most of the remaining furnishings, including screens, pulpit, benches and heavy studded door, are original. So are the graffiti in the porch which, says the guide, are 'such as are found in Pompeii and Rome'.

Staffordshire

Hoar Cross

HOLY ANGELS
Victorian memorial church in Decorated style

Hoar Cross is a masterpiece of the Gothic Revival. Bodley's early churches of the 1850s and 1860s, such as Selsley (Gloucs) and St Michael, Brighton (Sussex), were designed in a spare early French Gothic. Hoar Cross, of 1872, is from Bodley's middle period, when he had selected English late Decorated as the zenith of medieval architecture. Here, with his partner Thomas Garner, he developed the style to new heights, cramming his interior with liturgical paraphernalia. His client was Emily Meynell Ingram, daughter of Lord Halifax, whose husband of just seven years had been killed in a hunting accident. She commissioned the church both as his memorial and as a citadel of Anglo-Catholicism, to which Bodley was also attached.

The church lies at the entrance to the old house, now a health spa, into whose grounds the churchyard gently merges across a sunken garden. The exterior is a superb work of Decorated revival, comparing with Bodley's Clumber (Notts). The tower contrives to soar despite its lack of a spire. The graceful lines of the window mullions grow restless and break into furious Decorated tracery. The buttresses all have niche statues.

The inside is Victorian High Gothic with all the trimmings. This was intended as a church for remembering and worshipping, not for preaching. The gloom of the nave, which has no clerestory, leads the eye through the crossing and great screen to the chancel. This is taller than the nave and vaulted, lit by lofty windows, as though it were an ante-chamber to Heaven. Sedilia line both sides of the sanctuary, with the walls densely wrought with panelling and saints. More saints climb up the walls and windows, jostling with ballflower and nodding ogee arches, then spilling over into the stained glass. While Bodley and Garner collaborated on the architecture, the internal carving is mostly by Garner.

The stained glass is by Burlison & Grylls, but to Bodley's design. It depicts saints in soft colours that do not clash with the wood and stone carving. If stained glass there must be in an English parish church, it should have this sense of harmony. The stone reredos is magnificent.

The private chapel contains the tombs of Hugo and Emily. He lies under a sweeping ogee canopy, she under a flat wooden one, both on alabaster chests. Angels guard their heads, candles their feet. The ensemble is a superb display of wealthy Victorian piety.

Cheadle

ST GILES RC
Pugin's complete 13th-century re-creation

A. W. N. Pugin's St Giles, Cheadle is the outstanding English church of the 19th century. The patron was the 16th Earl of Shrewsbury who lived at the neighbouring mansion of Alton Towers. Shrewsbury was rich, liberal and a Roman Catholic. Pugin, also a Catholic and still only twenty-nine, was the architectural impresario of the day. The church commissioned in 1841 for the centre of Cheadle was intended to recreate the architecture of the pre-Reformation church. Since most of the churches in this book have their roots in the same religion, Cheadle shares their form and customary features. The difference is that at Cheadle they were recreated complete, in full colour and splendour. Cheadle was a reaction against both the classical architecture and sparse fittings of the Protestant church, and the frivolous Gothic of the Regency period.

The dark sandstone steeple can be seen from miles around, but within the town it rises as a sudden *coup de théâtre* at the foot of a hill off the High Street. The height is 200 ft and the proportion almost unbearably slender. But tresses, then pinnacles, then lucarnes cling to the sides of the spire, as if pleading with it to go no higher. Some spires seem reluctant to escape their towers. Cheadle does so joyfully. The west door is almost as dramatic as the steeple, the hinges formed into two huge Shrewsbury lions, covering each door in gold on a red background. Exterior niches are filled with the appropriate statues, including the two St Johns on the east wall.

The interior lacks nothing that the late 13th century would have included. The church has a standard plan with a nave, aisles, baptistery to the west and a chancel with chapels to the east. There is a screen with loft and rood, a Doom painting and saints in niches. In the chancel are an Easter Sepulchre, piscina, sedilia and reredos. The Doom includes the Earl's daughter, Gwendoline, on the right of Christ among those to be saved. Such was the power of patronage.

Not an inch of Cheadle is without paint, carving or gilding. Even the window reveals are meticulously decorated, each shaft picked out in different coloured patterns, like the leggings of a Carpaccio gondolier. Nor is there any restraint in the materials. The Lady Chapel screen is of brass, as are the candlesticks, the candelabra and even the step treads. The sedilia and Easter Sepulchre shimmer in reds, greens and gold. Coloured tiles from Wedgwood and Minton line the floor.

Decoration reaches crescendo in the south chancel chapel. Metal grilles and symbols of the Eucharist and Lamb of God are everywhere. The pulpit is carved from a single block of stone, the font from one of alabaster. Whether the decoration of a Gothic church of the 13th–14th centuries was truly as rich as this we cannot know. Certainly that was the belief of the Gothic revivalists. Glass mostly by William Wailes fills the windows. Piped church music fills the interior, and delightful too.

The only disappointment is the pews, dull and uncomfortable.

Suffolk

Framlingham

ST MICHAEL
16th-century Howard family mausoleum

Framlingham Castle is among the most picturesque in England, its towers and battlements riding majestically over the Suffolk landscape. Until the 17th century, it belonged to the Dukes of Norfolk, variously of the Mowbray and Howard lines. At the Dissolution, the 3rd Duke lost his ancestral mausoleum of Thetford Priory, and rebuilt the chancel at Framlingham church as the new resting place for his family's remains. He was condemned to death by Henry VIII, but was reprieved when the king died the day before the execution was due to take place. Though uncle of both Anne Boleyn and Catherine Howard and politically reckless, the Duke contrived to die in his bed in 1554. His new mausoleum served its purpose for only a few years, since in 1555 his son, the 4th Duke, married Mary Fitzalan and moved the family's principal seat to her home in Sussex. The tombs at Framlingham are thus from just three decades of the 16th century.

The church exterior is conventional Suffolk Perpendicular, though its tower has an unusually elaborate bell-opening. The flushwork of the clerestory and the pierced lead cresting of the roof are superb. Inside, this roof is no less sensational. The arch braces fall onto hammerbeams, but these are not revealed, being concealed behind an 'aisle' of wooden lierne vaults. This is not a roof of angels and fantasy, more one of virtuoso carpentry.

There is no escaping that this is a church remodelled as the shrine to a great family. Huge open chapels flank the chancel on both north and south sides. These house and celebrate the tombs that now stand splendidly restored and recoloured, offering an array of early classicism unique in England. They are rightly described by the guidebook as 'the last major display of religious imagery in England before the full weight of the Reformation theology made such things impossible'.

Much ink has been spilt over the dates of the four main 16th-century tombs, but the work is now thought to belong to two phases, the 1530s and the 1550s–60s. The effigies are not the strongest feature of the works, interest lying chiefly in the details of the tomb chests beneath them. The first tomb, south of the altar, belongs to the builder of the chapels, the 3rd Duke. The chest probably dates from the 1530s, with the effigies added in the 1550s. The design is unorthodox classical, thick with balusters, colonettes and double capitals. Yet the saints round the chest are grave figures beautifully carved in shell niches, true Renaissance forms.

Nearby is the tomb of Henry Fitzroy, son of Henry VIII by Catherine of Aragon's lady-in-waiting, Elizabeth Blount. He was created Duke of Richmond and married the 3rd Duke's daughter; alas for Norfolk's ambitions, he died aged seventeen in 1536. The tomb is more chaste and classical than the 3rd Duke's, with Ionic pilasters round the chest, and probably belongs to the mid-16th century. However, the reliefs round the top of the chest, showing scenes from Genesis, including the Expulsion from the Garden of Eden, are probably earlier work moved from Thetford.

The north chapel contains two monuments of a similar date. Against the wall is the small tomb of the infant daughter of the 4th Duke, Elizabeth (d.1565). It is a simple classical chest modelled on that of the Duke of Richmond, crowned by a Gothic ogee canopy presumably from a former monument. Also in this chapel is the tomb of the 4th Duke's two wives. Its classicism is much the most accomplished, with full columns round the chest, surmounted by beautifully carved consoles.

Next door, the style alters again with the 1614 tomb of an earlier Howard, the Earl of Surrey, beheaded in 1547. The proportions are exaggerated, effigies are boastful and architectural features heavy and distorted. Decorum was re-established with the acquisition of Framlingham from the Howards by Robert Hitcham in 1635. His tomb is a serene black marble slab of 1638, with no effigy and supported by kneeling angels. He lies in the south chapel, apparently happy to be overshadowed by his ducal surroundings.

Kedington

ST PETER AND ST PAUL
Unmodernised interior, Barnardiston tombs

Kedington comes in the top rank of small English churches. It offers nothing out of the ordinary, nothing jarring or shocking, just consistency of craftsmanship and the harmony of ages. On a sunny day we can sit in the churchyard and watch the shadows glide over tombstones and spread across the chancel wall, as they have done for centuries.

Inside no inch is without diversion. Nave and aisles contain every component of a parish church, tombs, screens, pews, altars, paintings, all tumbling out of the gloom. Overhead a hammerbeam roof is illuminated by strange skylights. The nave piers have 18th-century painted fluting. In each spandrel is a hatchment, most belonging to the local Barnardiston family, grandees of Kedington from the Middle Ages to the 18th century.

The seating forms an extraordinary collection, from small uncomfortable benches at the back to tall family pews at the front. The Barnardiston pew on the left is composed of the battered fragments of the old screen, complete with defaced saints. The tall three-decker pulpit still has its tester, candle, hour glass and wigstand.

At the back of the church is a set of raised children's pews with a boxed-in seat for the teacher, and next to them a musicians' gallery. A Jacobean screen of 1619 guards the chancel, but can be folded back on hinges.

The survival of all this in one place is remarkable. It is reminiscent of another Dickensian sort of church, that of Puddletown (Dorset).

The aisles are devoted to Barnardiston tombs, earlier in the south aisle, later in the north. They form a gallery of vernacular monuments from the Middle Ages to the Renaissance and on into the 18th century. There are Barnardistons of 1503, 1584, 1609 and 1610. None is of great quality and the early effigies are battered. The value is in the collection as a whole, a vivid evocation of dynasties past and glories gone. More tombs are in the Barnardiston vault, reached from behind the pulpit and reputedly containing up to fifty coffins. John Betjeman understandably christened Kedington 'a village Westminster Abbey'.

Long Melford

HOLY TRINITY
Richest East Anglian church, Clopton Chantry,
Lily Crucifix, medieval glass

One day we may honour towns created in the 20th century as we now honour Lavenham and Long Melford. For the time being, there is no contest. They both embody the informal yet graceful development of 16th- and 17th-century England. They were not planned, growing up round medieval streets as and when building was needed, yet today they seem all of a piece. Once among the richest towns in Europe, their churches reflected that wealth. Long Melford was blessed with three wool tycoons, the Cloptons of Kentwell, the Cordells of

Melford Hall and the Martyns of Melford Place. All left their mark on a church which is a treasure house of English medieval art.

Of a former church on the site, only the nave arcades survive, with piers and capitals of the 14th century. The remainder was rebuilt *c*.1490 under the ascendancy of John Clopton, the arcades being extended to nine bays. Clopton generosity is recalled throughout the church, with thirty-two members of the family honoured in the north aisle donors' windows. Other names associated with the building include Loveday, Boteler, Smyth, Hyll, Martyn and, as one inscription relates, 'all the well-disposed men of this town'. These donors so dominate the Melford story that we can never escape them.

Like its Cotswold contemporaries, Long Melford is almost all late Perpendicular, its excitement deriving from contents more than architecture. Nothing at Long Melford is hidden under a bushel. The exterior is stretched out on a rise at the edge of the town, a giant of flushwork, flint and glass. Tudor almshouses frame the churchyard approach. The original tower was destroyed by lightning, replaced in the 18th century and further encased in flint in 1903. The chancel displays a single lofty window embracing the clerestory, reminiscent of a Tudor banqueting hall. The Lady Chapel has steeply pitched roofs ending in three gables. It is the only chapel of such ambition attached to an English parish church – though Burford (Oxon) is similar – and is surrounded by a sunny ambulatory.

The interior is best appreciated by moving clockwise round the church from the north aisle. The surviving north window glass records a plutocracy that must have deterred even the most determined iconoclast. Second from the left is the 'Alice in Wonderland' glass of Elizabeth Talbot, said to have inspired John Tenniel's drawings for Lewis Carroll. Next to it is a glass of three rabbits sharing three ears, representing the Trinity. The remainder of the north aisle is a rollcall of kneeling donors and associated saints and heraldry, God and Mammon in magnificent unison.

At the east end of this aisle is the Kentwell Chapel. Here Sir William Clopton (d.1446), father of John, rests in prayer and calm serenity. Next door is an alabaster relief of the Adoration fixed to the wall, presumably recovered from a ruined reredos. This is the Clopton corner. Family brasses litter the floor. In the east wall is a double squint, cutting through both chapel and chantry wall for a glimpse of the high altar. A passage now leads east through a tiny priest's alcove, containing a fireplace and its own miniature fan vault, into John Clopton's private chantry.

The Clopton Chantry contrasts with the rest of the church. It is a small chapel with a continuous frieze of saints in niches, with, round the cornice, John Lydgate's 'Vine of Life' poem in the form of a scroll. The tomb of John Clopton (d.1497) stands in the wall between the chantry and main chancel. It has no effigies, but the vault of the canopy has faded portraits of him and his wife and a well-preserved Christ, apparently walking with a flowing cloak. The chapel east window contains an exquisite and now rare Lily Crucifix, depicting Christ on the leaves of a lily against a sky-blue background. The clear glass round it reveals a hollybush outside. This chapel would once have been a blaze of colour.

We now enter the chancel, and encounter the Cordell family and the Renaissance. Clopton was a merchant prince of the early Tudor period; Sir William Cordell (d.1580) was a new man, a lawyer-courtier to the Elizabethans. He was a judge and Speaker of the House of Commons. His entertainment of Elizabeth I at Melford Hall set a standard for extravagance that ruined numerous courtiers.

The century dividing Cordell's tomb from Clopton's could hardly be wider. Cordell may still lie in medieval armour with his hands in prayer, but above him rise the columns, coffered arches and Cardinal Virtues of classicism. Justice, Prudence, Temperance and Fortitude watch over him in Roman dress.

Balancing the Clopton Chapel on the south side of the chancel is the Martyn Chapel, notable for early family brasses. From here we reach the separate Lady Chapel. The building was used as a school after the Reformation and a multiplication table is preserved on the east wall. The chapel has the unusual form of a central sanctuary surrounded on four sides by an ambulatory. It is a happy, light-filled place with an old clock on the wall. Today it must be Britain's grandest Sunday school. The verges outside are lined in summer with giant hollyhocks, dancing attendance on well-clipped yews.

Southwold

ST EDMUND
Flint flushwork exterior, medieval choir stalls,
20th-century font cover

Southwold is the grandest of the galleons that once sailed the length of the Suffolk coast. It has survived while Walberswick, Covehithe and Dunwich disappeared or decayed. The mighty flint tower is an East Anglian classic and its porch a fitting companion. The proportion of tower to nave is harmonious, 100 ft to 144 ft. Nowhere in Suffolk is the subtle interplay of flushwork flint and stone better displayed. What the Somerset masons could fashion from sculpted stone, their Suffolk contemporaries fashioned in the marquetry of knapped flint.

Southwold church sits on the outskirts of the resort, surrounded by a spacious close, and seems to affirm permanence on a constantly shifting coast. The west front is a glory of flushwork. Panelling rises up each buttress, dado and niche. Chequerboard courses and a pseudo-pierced parapet are all created flush with the wall. Round the west window is the simple inscription which translates from the Latin as 'Saint Edmund Pray For Us', each letter under a flushwork crown.

The porch speaks the same language. It has chequerboard stone and flint on its battlements. Two Perpendicular windows light the south wall of the upper chamber and a modern statue of St Edmund fills the niche. The porch is vaulted and the door, with linenfold panelling, is original.

The interior is a hymn to light, enhanced by the clear glass in the windows and by sensitive restoration. Nothing jars. The 19th- and 20th-century work, so often offensive, here preserves or recreates a stylistic whole, essentially that of the late 15th century. The roof alternates arched braces and angels on hammerbeams. As they reach the chancel area, the angels change from monochrome to vivid colouring, their feathers spread beneath a sky of blue and golden stars.

Below is a forest of screens. The chancel screen has no tracery, the decoration being carried on the painted uprights and the cusped arches. The saints are excellently painted. The 1870s retouching is said to be 'diffident', though Norman Scarfe in the *Shell Guide* remarks that St Jude was made to seem 'very much like the rector'.

Southwold's choir stalls are among the best in Suffolk, rich especially in their arm-rests, poppyheads and canopies. The rests include finely carved animals and a man with toothache. The benches display the initials of boys who used this as a school until the 19th century.

The present quality of the furnishings owes much to the work of Comper's pupil, F. E. Howard, who visited the church in the 1920s and declared it a 'model of an English church after the Book of Common Prayer'. Howard was an authority on woodwork. He designed the reredos and lectern and restored the 15th-century pulpit. His chief contribution is the font cover. This dwarfs even that of Ufford. It takes off like a rocket, rising 24 ft to be the highest in any English parish church. Next to it stands Southwold Jack, a medieval clock 'smiter' in 15th-century costume.

Southwold possesses a walnut chest covered in intricate tracery and depicting a knight hunting a boar. Those who worry at the plight of the Church of England might note that, when Defoe visited this community in 1722, he found just twenty-seven people in the church, and over 600 Dissenters worshipping elsewhere.

Warwickshire

Stratford-upon-Avon

HOLY TRINITY
Perpendicular chancel, Clopton Chapel,
Shakespeare's tomb

Were the name of Stratford not associated with a certain
playwright, it would be noted for its church. Holy Trinity
stands with St Mary, Warwick as one of the glories of
the county. It is peacefully away from the town's centre,
up river from the theatre and the main Shakespearean
attractions. From the river walk, the chancel rises ghostly
white on the bank, a pavilion of stone and glass with
enriched window surrounds. From the churchyard, the
impression is different, of a solid Early Gothic and Decorated tower and 18th-century spire, and transepts with
Decorated windows. In the churchyard is a fine avenue
of pollarded limes, as in many churchyards representing
biblical tribes and apostles.

The church welcomes tourists seeking Shakespeare's
tomb, and reasonably requests a small fee to enter the
chancel to see it; there is no charge for the rest of the
church. The aisle windows display a variety of Decorated
tracery, maybe due to wayward masons or wayward
patrons. The south aisle is the more ornate, being the
chapel of Stratford's college of St Thomas. Its corbels

include a monstrous bull. The college prospered in the 15th century and was responsible in 1480 for the rebuilding of the chancel and nave clerestory, hence the soaring nave superstructure of vertical panelling and twelve windows each side. The roof has bosses and the tie-beams rest on little castellated corbels. The view east is given added drama by a Victorian *coup de théâtre*, the organ case by Bodley above the crossing arch, carved with tracery and crockets, a tremendous Gothic flourish.

In the nave is the dark green and white marble pulpit donated by an Edwardian benefactor, Sir Theodore Martin, in honour of his wife, the actress Helen Faucit. She is said to be depicted in the carving of St Helena. Behind Tudor screens in the north aisle lies the Clopton Chapel. This was built for Hugh Clopton who, like many medieval clothiers, grew rich, moved to the City of London, became Lord Mayor and was buried there in 1496. His tomb chest therefore stands empty and the chapel houses a number of his less eminent descendants.

William Clopton (d.1592) and his wife lie against the north wall. He is armoured, in medieval fashion, and both hold small prayer books. Behind are their children, those who died at birth wrapped in swaddling clothes. The adjacent tomb of their son-in-law, George Carew, Earl of Totnes (d.1629), is a fine composition by Edward Marshall, chief mason to Charles II. Carew was Master in Ordnance for James I and the emblems of his office decorate the chest. The guide reports this as 'the finest Renaissance tomb in Europe', a bold claim.

Stratford's chancel 'weeps' to the north. It is as glorious within as without. North and south walls are filled with transomed Perpendicular windows, niches and memorials. The roof angels hold shields of Warwickshire families; the niche statues on the east wall are supported on giant insects. Under the choir stalls, misericords include the popular depiction of a wife beating her husband, pulling his beard and kicking his crotch, as well as a naked woman riding a stag.

Shakespeare's tomb is by the sanctuary rail, with its famous curse: 'Bleste be the man that spares these stones, and curst be he that moves my bones.' Above is the 'sunburnt' portrayal of him by Gerard Johnson, a memorial sculpted for his wife shortly after his death in 1616 and thus said to be the most plausible likeness. It has the half-length bust popular at the time for scholars. He gazes benignly out at his admirers, quill and paper in hand. Barely a line in the guidebook omits his name. We see the font in which he would have been baptised, the Bible he would have heard read and the register of his birth and his death.

Wiltshire

Devizes

ST JOHN
Norman chancel carving, 15th-century chantries

Devizes is my first choice as the quintessential English country town. It lies beneath the Wiltshire Downs, its name derived from 'ad divisas', or the division of two regions. The parish church stands over a small valley from the castle, both created in *c*.1130 by Roger, Bishop of Salisbury and Chancellor to Henry I. He might still recognise them. St John's lies down a medieval lane behind the town hall, framed by an old gate and lamp-bracket. The scene is closed by the heavy Norman crossing tower and north transept.

The east end should first be inspected from outside. Here Roger's original chancel east wall survives with its windows and buttresses. While most chancels were rebuilt and embellished in the Gothic period, Devizes was for some reason overlooked. By the 15th century, the laity were dominating church patronage and their interest was not in spending money on chancels. At Devizes the Beauchamp and Lamb families donated chantries for the sake of their own souls. These stand on either side of the chancel, which is left as a poor relation sandwiched in between. Of the two chantries,

Beauchamp is the more ostentatious, with lofty pinnacles, carved battlements, panelled buttresses and an
ornamental priest's door. Beauchamps were rarely
outshone

The interior of St John's is an essay in stylistic contrast, between Perpendicular nave and Norman chancel.
The former is refined and English, the latter brash and
French, two nations in not altogether happy juxtaposition, joined by a chancel arch above which hang
two flags as if of two monarchs. (They are Wiltshire's
regimental colours.) The 'English' nave is heavily
restored, graceful but rather mass-produced. Its best
feature is the set of corbel faces in the aisles. There is no
clerestory, making the interior gloomy on a dark day.

The 'French' chancel wins the day, tunnel-like, a stage-
set for a Norman drama of incense, hooded monks and
drawn swords. Seen from the nave, it is a forest of shafts,
rising to a low rib vault. This frames the extraordinary
east end, a riotous tableau of blind arcading, intersecting
arches and zigzag carving. The poppyheads on the choir
stalls stand to attention in the foreground.

The two side chapels bring us back to the 15th century.
Their ceilings are of a Moorish refinement and their
windows are ablaze with glass. The north, Lamb, chantry
is now a vestry, but the south, Beauchamp, chapel of the
same 1480s date forms a florid contrast to the Norman
work, with its panelled arches and 5-light traceried
windows. A reminder of the Normans are the corbel
heads surviving high on the north wall. These carvings,
of Kilpeck (Herefs) grotesqueness, would previously
have been outside the old church. They smirk down on

the effete Tudor rosettes, angels and saints like devils peeping in on Heaven.

The glass in St John's is mostly awful, but the organ case in the north transept is a 17th-century masterpiece, in the style of Grinling Gibbons.

Malmesbury

THE ABBEY
Romanesque figure sculpture, King Athelstan's tomb

Seen from the north across the Avon, Malmesbury sits like a ruined galleon. Holes gape in its superstructure, turrets are gaunt in the wind, flanks bear the scars of old battles. Yet from the town side the view is totally different. A close unfolds gracefully from the high street. Across the churchyard rises the large porch inside which is one of England's outstanding compositions of Anglo-Norman art.

The church lies in the remains of a Benedictine abbey whose spire was once as high as that of Salisbury. The abbey church was built *c.*1170, but its crossing tower collapsed in the early 16th century, destroying the chancel and crossing. Then in the 17th century the Gothic west tower fell, taking with it the three west bays of the nave. This fall was catastrophic and what survives today is a truncated section of the Norman nave. Approaching from the south, we can clearly see the relics of the old west front and the fragments of the south transept.

But there is still the famous porch. The outer entrance has a Norman portal of eight arches, including three of sculptured reliefs set in roundels. These depict the

Creation and scenes from the Old Testament and from the Life of Christ. Such stories were often portrayed in wall paintings or stained glass. Here they are executed in stone. The inner doorway is crowned with a tympanum showing Christ on a rainbow supported by angels in a flowing embrace. Even more remarkable is the carving along the interior walls of the porch, six on each side portraying the apostles at Pentecost, with an angel flying overhead. They are shown seated in exaggerated poses with sinuous draperies. St Peter has had his feet knocked off by iconoclasts, to prevent worshippers from kissing them. These are big, highly expressive works which Pevsner relates to Burgundian work of *c*.1130. They are great treasures in what is now the parish church of a small town.

The interior is a lovable hybrid. The surviving arcades are late Norman, with multi-scalloped capitals, cylindrical piers and slightly pointed arches. Above is a splendid Norman gallery. A few splashes of naturalistic foliage on the capitals of the wall shaft mark the point at which the later, Decorated Gothic, builders took over, adapting the clerestory and constructing a lierne vault. The vault has magnificent bosses, some human but most foliage, recently repainted. Looking down from the south gallery is an abbot's oratory, like an opera box.

The abbey's proudest possession is the tomb of the Saxon King Athelstan (d.939), grandson of Alfred the Great. He is acknowledged as first king of all the Britons, achieved by defeating both the Scots and the Norsemen of York. The monument is Perpendicular, though the head and the lion are later replacements. A stone screen in the south aisle encloses the chapel of another famous scion of Malmesbury, the 8th-century St Aldhelm. He was a scholar and writer of Latin riddles who owned, so it was said, a finer library even than the Venerable Bede. He was beneficiary of the Roman Abbot Hadrian's visit to Britain in 668, which led to the revival of Roman studies at Canterbury, whence Aldhelm came to Malmesbury as abbot.

Above the porch is a museum of some of the abbey's treasures. These include illuminated manuscripts and prints of the abbey at various stages of its decay and restoration. In the south aisle is an unusual Burne-Jones window made after his death by Morris & Co. It portrays Faith, Courage and Devotion in glamorous armour against a background of green lozenges. Another window celebrates England's earliest aviator, an 11th-century monk named Elmer. He made himself wings, took off from one of the abbey towers and broke both his legs.

Worcestershire

Great Malvern

THE PRIORY CHURCH
Hillside setting, Norman nave arcades,
medieval wall tiles and stained glass

The former Benedictine priory of Great Malvern, now
the parish church, nestles cosily in a fold of the Malvern
Hills. It is nearly invisible until we are upon it, when it
erupts like a volcano from the side of the hill. The tower
and exterior are of extraordinary richness. Even the
turrets on the tower battlements have pierced finials.
Night-time floodlights throw the tower panelling into
relief and offer a superb display of Perpendicular grandeur, from the chancel to the theatrical north porch. And
this is just the setting. Malvern contains some of the
finest medieval glass in England, to rank with that at
Ludlow (Salop) and Fairford (Gloucs).

The first impression of the nave interior comes as a
shock after the exterior. The arcades are severely Norman, the cylindrical piers rising to unadorned capitals
and arches. The walls above are of solid masonry, more
Cistercian than Benedictine. Only in the Perpendicular
clerestory are we granted some of the light of day.
The nave roof is a George Gilbert Scott recreation of a
15th-century original. The eye, however, is swiftly drawn

eastwards. There are no screens in Malvern and the volume of the nave continues through the vaulted and panelled crossing into the chancel, to reach a climax in the great east window. This is a tunnel of architecture.

Once reached, the chancel is a complete contrast to the nave. It is in panelled Perpendicular, its walls little more than decorative frames for the windows and, like the tower, influenced by Gloucester Cathedral. Beneath are medieval choir stalls with superb misericords. These include an almost complete set of the Labours of the Months, forming a parade of medieval secular life.

Also in the chancel is the alabaster memorial to John Knotsford (d.1589), one of the beneficiaries of the Dissolution of the priory. He respected the church, and his daughter was proud to have him commemorated here. Malvern's unique collection of medieval wall tiles, the largest in the country, adorns the rear of the screens round the sanctuary.

Now for the glass. I know of no church which so well displays the majesty as well as ʰhe intimacy of medieval glazing. From a distance, the effect is kaleidoscopic rather than narrative, a shimmering refraction of pure colour. Malvern's glass dates from the end of the 15th century, the colouring soft and complex and slightly earlier than that at Fairford. Some of the original background has gone and there is much Victorian repair and insertion, so that sometimes the theme of each window is clear, sometimes a jumble of restoration. But the intention is intact, of presenting biblical and other scenes in a strong architectural framework.

Of the dominant east window, a third is thought to

be original. Much is jumbled, but the Crucifixion and apostles are clear. The north transept window contains an exceptionally rare depiction of the Coronation of Mary (particular target of iconoclasts) in a wide halo of blue sky with stars. This gift to the priory by Henry VII was designed by the royal glaziers in 1501. The glass in the south chancel aisle is of Old Testament scenes and includes the much reproduced Expulsion and the Burning Bush. The west window is also medieval and is a copy of the east window at Exeter Cathedral.

Malvern's glass has been the subject of much study, to which the bookshop supplies an admirable guide.

Great Witley

ST MICHAEL
Gibbs interior, Georgian painted glass,
Rysbrack monument

Every church has its moment. I caught Great Witley on a wild December evening with the sun setting over the wooded hills to the west. It might have been in Transylvania. The vast ruin of the old house next door was already filling with nocturnal ghosts. The church, in the midst of Evensong, was a casket of light and sound. I saw coloured glass as it is rarely seen, lit from the inside at dusk to the accompaniment of a choir.

Witley Court was created by the Foleys, early ironmasters, in the 17th century. In the 1730s it was expanded for Thomas Foley and a new church was built next door. Determined to do it proud, he imported the fittings, pictures and windows bought at the famous 1747 auction of the Duke of Chandos's Canons estate in Edgware. The old village was moved a mile away to the present Great Witley. Foleys went and Dudleys came, and Victorian Witley became one of the most spectacular mansions in the Midlands. But all fortunes wane. Witley was sold in 1920 and in 1937 a fire rendered the house uninhabitable. Its contents were plundered by vandals and it is now in the care of English Heritage.

The church survived through the care of the once-spurned villagers, for this was never just the preserve of the big house but always the local parish church. The architecture, by an unknown hand, is Baroque, with cupola, urns and balustrades bold against the skyline, and windows flanked by pilasters. This hardly prepares us for the Italianate extravaganza inside. Great Witley possesses the only full scheme of Baroque decoration of any church in England, certainly outside London.

The interior is the work of James Gibbs and reflects his training in Rome under Carlo Fontana, the leading Baroque architect of the day. Walls and ceiling are covered in lavish gilded relief decoration. Although it looks like stucco it is mostly of papier-mâché, a technique employed to reduce weight across so wide a ceiling. The craftsmen were Italians, who worked extensively in English country houses in the early 18th century. Set into the ceiling are paintings on canvas by Antonio Bellucci. The central panel shows the Resurrection in dramatic foreshortening. It is as if Christ were struggling to ascend from the roof of Great Witley itself.

The ten windows depicting Bible scenes came from Canons. They were possibly by another Italian, Francisco

Slater, although executed in enamel and signed by a York-shireman, Joshua Price. They arrived by wagon in 38 sections and form a complete biblical narrative round the church, the best collection of 18th-century glass extant. The benches, font cover and pulpit are Victorian but were intended to complement the Baroque above, replacing more staid Georgian predecessors. The organ case is a Canons original and seems about to burst forward from the west wall. It was one of the instruments at which Handel is believed to have played his Chandos anthems.

We turn almost in relief to the gigantic Rysbrack memorial to the 1st Lord Foley, completed in 1735 and thus before the fitting out of the church. The cost was an astonishing £2,000. It is reputedly the tallest such monument in England and is a masterpiece of the genre. The conventional obelisk is crowded with tiers of figures, their poses and flowing costumes completing the Baroque effect.

Pershore

THE ABBEY
Early Gothic chancel vault, crossing tower lantern
and monuments

Pershore is a pretty town on the banks of the Avon, its former abbey set back from the Georgian main street across a wide green. From the outside it might be just another Dissolution fragment, a ghost of past majesty left for the benefit of the townspeople. But here the Reformers at least left not a nave but a chancel, with a sumptuous crossing and tower.

Norman Pershore was of the same period and stylistic group as Gloucester and Tewkesbury, that is begun within a generation of the Conquest. The exterior shows scattered dogtooth, a Norman corbel-table on the south transept, blind arcading and a pair of vigorous 20th-century buttresses to keep it all upright. The tower is later, with Decorated bell-openings and pinnacles. So too is the chancel, with its lofty lancet windows and effete Victorian apse.

Pershore's interior is superlative, one of the most beautiful in the county. The inside of the tower was opened up in George Gilbert Scott's 1860s restoration so that the internal stone panelling could be seen. To Scott, Pershore's lantern was bettered only at Lincoln. He replaced the old ringing-chamber with a platform floating in space, reached by a spiral staircase. It looks surreal.

The south transept is substantially Norman, but its interest lies in the monuments. These include the tombs of a knight and an abbot and, against the west wall, a strangely elongated memorial to Thomas Haselwood. The charity boards are of unusual detail. One refuses charity to any 'who are given to excessive drinking, or are whoremongers, common swearers or pilferers or otherwise scandalous'. This must have excluded many candidates.

The chancel was rebuilt in the Early Gothic style after a fire destroyed the Norman chancel in 1223. Its principal beauty lies in its arcades and high clerestory, and in the richness of the lierne vault, erected half a century later at the dawn of the Decorated period. The triple shafts of the clerestory arches embrace a wall passage below the windows. The vault ribs rise from shafts beginning in the spandrels of the main arcades, themselves composed of luxuriant clusters of shafts. The effect is of a soaring forest of ribs.

The capitals are superb, displaying a variety of stiff-leaf, some of it wrought into knots, some 'windblown', all a delight to the eye. No less dazzling are the star-patterned vaults, the liernes creating scissor shapes and given 'ploughshare twists' for 3-D effect. The bosses include Green Men and a 'laughing boss'. They are hard to see against a scraped ceiling that yearns for limewash.

The east wall of the church was restored by Scott who inserted an apse. His thin Victorian east lancet thus enjoys a dominant position, pointing upwards to a triple lancet above. The insertion is entirely successful, new architecture enhancing old. Perhaps a future generation will open the upper windows to complete the clerestory circuit. There is so much adjustment of this sort, which need not be controversial, awaiting restorers in English churches.

In the south aisle are windows by John Hardman, tracing Pershore's history, culminating in a depiction of Queen Victoria. This is the best sort of narrative glass, unashamedly medieval in style and set in a dominant blue.

Yorkshire

Bolton Abbey

ST MARY AND ST CUTHBERT
Early Gothic doorway, botanical reredos

Bolton shares with Fountains Abbey a landscape as picturesque as any in England. Ruskin's verbose account is often quoted: 'Noble moorlands extend above, purple with heath and broken into scars and glens . . . an instinctive apprehension of the strength and greatness of the wild northern land. It is to the association of this power and border sternness with the sweet peace and tender decay of Bolton Priory that the scene owes its distinctive charm.' The ensemble of house, village, park and priory is immaculately conserved.

The history of the Augustinian priory is important. The east end of the church, including its crossing, transepts and choir, decayed after the Dissolution and is now a ruin. A new west tower begun in 1520 by the last prior, Prior Moone, was left unfinished and the Early Gothic nave behind it was converted in 1539 into a parish church. Bolton, like Milton Abbey (Dorset), was a grandiose monastic project cut short by the Reformation, with the local parish given whatever the masons had completed so far. What we see today is an archaeological curiosity, half ruin, half unfinished tower, set amid lawns, trees and the slopes of distant hills. The west tower was intended to be spectacular, judging by the two huge buttresses and a west window that is crowned with an ogee arch that now rises impressively into space.

This tower base has been given a modern roof and bell-turret, and forms an entrance porch which also protects the old 13th-century west front. 'A historical calamity,' says the guide, 'has been transformed into a glorious antechamber to the House of God.' The doorway is a masterpiece of Early Gothic design, its clustered shafts and chamfered arches rising to a beauti-fully balanced point. The doorway is surrounded by blind arcading which covers every part of the elevation. Even the door hinges are lovely works of what I call Gothic rococo.

The interior, despite the loss of the east end, is most satisfying. To the south runs a sequence of six Early Gothic twinned lancets, embellished with dogtooth and filled with A. W. N. Pugin glass. They tell the Life of Christ in 36 panels, within a controlled swirl of abstract patterns that form a wall of light and colour. The north arcade opposite is of four giant bays with deep-set but spacious clerestory windows above. At the west end of this north aisle is a brilliantly coloured small window depicting St Cuthbert.

The sanctuary is Victorian, with as backdrop the east wall inserted at the Reformation to fill the old crossing arch. It was rebuilt by Street in 1877 and is dominated by his stone panelled reredos. This was painted by two local craftsmen, Thomas Bottomley and his apprentice, R. G. Greenwood. It depicts Pre-Raphaelite Madonna lilies, alternating with symbolic biblical plants, barley, olive, vine, passion flower, rose and palm. It forms a wonderful climax to the interior but was once considered too secular and was covered with a curtain. The dark Perpendicular roof is alive with golden angels. One of the bosses is a gruesome Green Man, with one branch emerging from his mouth, the other from his eye.

Lastingham

ST MARY
Norman crypt with ancient capitals

The crypt at Lastingham is among England's special places. I first visited it on a damp autumn evening when the moor outside was cold and still. Solitude itself had crept inside the church, descended to the crypt and knelt to pray.

The ghosts were those of the age of Bede, St Cedd, St Chad and the earliest missionaries to the north. On a small lectern I found Eliot's stern lines: 'You are here to kneel where prayer has been valid . . . Here the intersection of the timeless moment is England and nowhere. Never and always.' Some churches are a challenge to the faithful; Lastingham is a challenge to the faithless.

The church lies in a picturesque fold in the North York Moors. A monastery of Lastingham was founded by St Cedd in 654 as an outpost of Bishop Aidan's at Lindisfarne. The following year St Cedd travelled south to found the surviving church of Bradwell (Essex) and was succeeded as abbot by his brother St Chad. It was abandoned during the Viking period, rebuilt after the Conquest with the present crypt dedicated to St Cedd, but deserted again in 1088. Lastingham has been a parish church since the 13th century.

The crypt is unique in England in its complexity, having two aisles, a small chancel and an apse. It is reached down steps from the nave and is low and cell-like. The Norman piers and capitals in the crypt are like dwarfs with the heads of grown men. The 11th-century carvers of these capitals knew the relics of the Roman empire. They knew the classical orders even if they interpreted them freely, for instance taking Ionic volutes and turning them into rams' horns. This is the most intriguing of all architectural transitions: Norman Romanesque at its most Roman.

The main church presents different exterior aspects. When seen from the east and below, it is of massive proportions. From the west, the higher west end is more domestic and has a Perpendicular tower. The interior is composed of the 11th-century aisled chancel and crossing. The nave planned at that time was never constructed, and instead the crossing is closed by a west wall erected in the 13th century. Yet the sequence of arcades and arches progressing towards the eastern apse is spectacular, enhanced by Pearson in his 19th-century restoration. He added groin vaults and clerestory lancets.

Lastingham has few furnishings of interest. It does not need them.

Selby

THE ABBEY
Norman nave, chancel stiff-leaf, east window tracery
with medieval glass

Selby is subordinate only to Beverley Minster (Yorks, ER) and York Minster among the giants of Yorkshire. Comparing Selby and Beverley is one of the joys of English church visiting. Beverley's glory is promiscuous and loud. Selby's is that of a stately old lady, retired to the country with her dignity and memories intact.

Like York, Selby rests on just 3 ft of sand above the water table. This has led to tower settlement, drastically distorting the arches of the nave. The early builders had to let the structure settle on beams of wood sunk into the water. As a result, the centre of the abbey suffered extensive collapse in the 17th century. The roof was also destroyed in a fire in 1906, when the bells in the central tower melted and poured in a molten stream down into the church. A vast operation of reconstruction took place, including stone cleaning both inside and out. Today's church is in excellent condition.

Seen from the road to the south, its nave and Norman tower are low and powerful. To the east the sacristy and chancel erupt in a forest of 14th-century buttresses, pinnacles and flowing tracery, culminating in the famous Decorated east window. This is a swirl of flamboyant tracery, losing discipline as it rises and finding order only in the tulip-shaped oval at the top.

To the west beyond the nave stands the serene group

of west front and towers, the lower storey Norman, the upper Early Gothic and the rather stumpy towers Victorian. The facade is divided from Selby market place by a small parking area, trees and a lawn. It would benefit hugely by having the market extended directly to the foot of the abbey and the west door opened to the public. The planning of England's small towns is too aloof: the Italians and French handle these things better.

Selby's nave interior is Norman and Early Gothic, a mighty work of eight bays rising in three tiers, becoming later as we move westwards, and upwards.

The alternating piers are unmistakably copied from Durham Cathedral. The two eastern shafts have trellis decoration. The capitals throughout are rich and varied, scalloped, figurative, moulded and foliate. The north gallery is Transitional with water-leaf capitals and detached shafts. The south gallery and clerestory are Early Gothic. In the final bays the carvers can contain themselves no longer and burst into water-leaf. The post-fire roof includes a number of bosses saved from the wreckage. One can see why Pevsner regarded the Selby nave as 'to be warmly recommended to students'.

The chancel is Decorated and dates from the late 13th and early 14th centuries. The piers are adorned with elaborate foliage capitals, the leaves deeply undercut but tightly bunched, as at Patrington (Yorks, ER). Here the leaves are ubiquitous, turning aisles and arcades into arbours of vegetation. The arcade spandrels carry saints standing to attention. Above them rise a clerestory and passage adorned with carving and ogival arches. The roof begins on stone springers, but soon turns to wood and carries heavy gold bosses at its ridge.

All this is but a guard of honour for the chancel's east window, whose extraordinary tracery we noted outside. The work is more remarkable for retaining its medieval glass. Though much restored and with numerous Victorian surrounds to the original images, Selby's Tree of Jesse window is a masterpiece of English stained glass. It was saved from the 1906 fire when, at the last moment, the wind changed direction. Today it glows with a different fire, that of medieval artistry living on into the present day.

The chancel sedilia, four in number, are works of soaring filigree stonework. They have been attributed to the celebrated architect of early Perpendicular, Henry Yevele. The font cover of a similar date and design was luckily rescued from the fire. Stalls and other furnishings at Selby were not so fortunate. The awful chairs should be removed from the nave when not in use.

Studley Royal

ST MARY
Joyful Burges in Fountains Abbey setting

The church that William Burges built in 1870–8 for the Marquess and Marchioness of Ripon may not be to every taste, but for those who hold that the Victorians at their best were the equal of the 13th and 14th centuries, Studley Royal is a masterpiece. It sits at the far end of the landscaped estate of Fountains Abbey, now owned by the National Trust, closing the central avenue of what remains the definitive work of 18th-century English picturesque. The house has gone, so Burges's steeple must carry the climax to the composition. It does so with panache.

Landowners everywhere were erecting churches in the 1860s and 1870s. Lady Ripon was daughter of Lady Mary Vyner (and sister of the murdered boy at neighbouring Skelton). She commissioned the architect working for her mother, albeit to a more cheerful task. Lord Ripon was, or was to become, Viceroy of India, Grand Master of the Freemasons and an early Christian Socialist. He also converted to Roman Catholicism. Lady Ripon was the moving spirit behind the church, on which £50,000 was to be spent. The foundation stone was laid in the same year, 1870, as Skelton but the church was not opened until 1878. Burges was a gentleman architect with a private income and time to spend on detail. He was not racing from commission to commission like Scott, Street or Pearson and enjoyed working for a few grand patrons, such as the Butes in South Wales and the Ripons in Yorkshire. He was not a devout man and his approach to Gothic was, as the guide says, 'romantic, visual and scholastic rather than moral'.

The exterior is in Burges's familiar muscular style. At night, the silhouette against the sky can seem like a giant rhinoceros, with the tower as its horn. The building is heavily buttressed, the chancel windows enriched and the doors emboldened with splendid Gothic ironwork.

The interior is one of Burges's most successful compositions. The nave is a study in white stone and black Purbeck marble. Colour comes from the glass, not garish or over-elaborate and admitting enough light to give depth to Burges's shadows. Facing each other across the nave are the great organ, always a Burges speciality, reached by a spiral staircase, and the memorial tomb to the Marquess, executed in the finest marbles.

The chancel bursts into colour. Its dominant feature is the window tracery on two planes, possibly inspired by the Angel Choir at Lincoln Cathedral. The walls have shafts using differing marbles and are adorned with murals. The theme of the decorative scheme is the Book of Revelation. The sanctuary has an extraordinary gilded and painted dome with imagery of angels, music, trumpets, glory and Heaven. The floor mosaics depict the Garden of Eden and the building of Jerusalem. Not an inch is left undecorated, and there is a great rose window as a climax in the east wall.

The building is best seen with bright sunlight streaming through Burges's glass and dancing with the angels on his walls. The church, reached by a footpath across the park, is in the care of English Heritage.